CHRISTIAN HERITAGE COLLEGE
2100 Greenfield Dr.
El Cajon, CA 92021

LANGUAGE AND BELIEF

Jean Ladrière

LANGUAGE AND BELIEF

Translated by Garrett Barden

University of Notre Dame Press

American edition 1972

UNIVERSITY OF NOTRE DAME PRESS

Notre Dame, Indiana 46556

First published 1972 by

Gill and Macmillan Ltd

Originally published as *L'articulation du sens: discours scientifique et parole de la foi* in the series *Bibliotheque de Sciences Religieuses* edited by Michel de Certeau.

International Standard Book Number: 0–268–00479–x

Library of Congress Catalog Card Number: 72–3506

Printed and bound in the Republic of Ireland

Contents

Preface

I WISH to thank very sincerely the *Cahiers Internationaux de Symbolisme*, the Centre Catholique des Intellectual Francais, the Editions Aubiers-Montaigne, the Editions Desclée De Brouwer, the *Revue des Questions Scientifiques* and the *Tijdschrift voor Filosofie*, who have generously permitted the re-issue of the essays in this collection. I am grateful too to Père Michel de Certeau who not only accepted these essays for the *Bibliothèque des Sciences Religieuses* but also gave me every assistance in the preparation of the text.

Jean Ladrière

Introduction

THE essays in this collection were written in various circumstances more as answers to problems set by specific contexts
(symposia or talks) than as an effort to give unified form to a
determinate intention. Yet as it happens they all emerge
from a common problematic and from within a shared
perspective.

For a long time now faith has been questioning itself.
More exactly, reason, in the believer, questions faith and
requires some solution to its question. For, as compared
with the most intrinsic capacity of reason, which is to
constitute a discourse capable of furnishing, from its own
resources, its own justification, faith represents another
approach which must be at least understood, situated and,
in a sense, justified. This demand on reason's part is not of
necessity condemned to remain external to faith. It would
seem that faith, although it constitutes itself in its proper
domain with an evidence requiring no extrinsic support,
yet includes a demand for self-comprehension which,
fundamentally, is the unfolding of its proper mode of
evidence, but which must be articulated in an appropriate
discourse, and, on this basis, calls on the resources of
articulation which generates discourse. So the growth of
faith leads it to recollect in itself the question which reason
raises in respect of it.

But how understand faith without withdrawing oneself
from it, and how withdraw from it without destroying it?
One could mention here the peculiar character of the

reflexive act which is at once coincidence with itself and distance from itself, which never ceases to remain with itself in the operation by which it withdraws from itself. But how can reflexion assist us? Is it quite certain that in reflexion the mind can appear to itself in the totality of its content or even in a privileged part of its life? Is there an effective presence of experience in the recollection that the reflexive operation pretends to? For this to be in fact the case the reflexive operation must be able to disclose a foundational instance which would posit the content of experience in a simple act which encloses in itself the whole complexity of the lived experience. Even on the supposition that such a foundational instance could be, in principle, evoked, would it allow an appearing to self of such clarity as to justify a reflexive foundation of experience? For it seems that every effort which aims at a direct grasp of the operations constituting experience either ends with an empty form (which is no more than the indication of a possible experience) or with a pure state of self-consciousness which yields no more than a pin-point presence devoid of all fertility. Consequently, not a great deal can be expected, it seems, of an effort to understand faith in the very act of its effectuation. But then are we not condemned to reaching faith only from the outside, that is through institutions, gestures, modes of behaviour, which are not faith but merely its manifestations. The study of these manifestations could only be empirical and, without a correct understanding of faith itself, it would not be possible to discern their specificity. Faith is an experience. How reach an experience in what is only its traces in documents, inscriptions, objects?

In order to reach the experience in its content while at the same time remaining faithful to its truth as experience, one has to devise a means which will allow the unification of the interiority of the act with the exteriority of an objectifiable datum. Put another way we must have an objectification of experience which can be grasped as manifestation. Now language answers to precisely this problem since it is made of signs and a sign unites a perceptible phenomenon with a signification. As is clear from contemporary linguistics, language relates a phonological component (which is projected on the perceptible level in sounds adapted to the receptivity of the human ear) with a semantic component (forming a system of significations), by the intermediary of a formal organisation obeying determinate generative laws (the syntactic component). Certainly signification itself to the extent that it is inserted into a system is an objectivisable reality. The analysis of language can accordingly develop entirely on the level of exteriority. But to the extent that it is a process of articulation and exteriorisation of meaning it can become the carrier of an intention of signification and communication. Thus the reflexive approach, which is deceptive, can be replaced by the study of the objective forms in which experience organises itself. It is not a question of reconstructing the acts hidden behind the forms of language, but of disclosing, on the level of the modes of linguistic functioning, the structure of signifying life, and so of understanding consciousness in its content.

The linguistic approach will allow us catch the experience of faith in its objective aspect without for all that reducing the experience to a system of objects devoid of any intentionality. The language in which faith expresses itself is not a pure exteriority, a reality which can be reached only as a physical event. Because it is language, it is manifestation, in an objectively perceptible form, of that which makes faith an experience with its own specificity, its own organisation, its own differentiating and constitutive elements.

The study of the language of faith must be placed in the context of a study of language in general. On a first level, which should be foundational with respect to other levels whose possibility it should disclose, the traits characteristic of language will be assembled, and the general laws of its functioning will be discovered. Scientific linguistics is concerned with this enquiry. Its objective is not simply to analyse the mechanisms at work in the many extant natural languages but to discover the most general principles according to which all languages are organised and that not only the natural languages but also the 'artificial' languages invented to meet the needs of logical research or information technology. These principles have to maintain their validity not only for extant languages but for all possible languages. The guiding hypothesis here is that every language is essentially operative and that, consequently, it can be described by a system of rules. The rules in question are not just any rules whatsoever; they must meet certain general conditions that are found in every particular system of rules (that is in every concrete language) and whose power is to make language precisely what it is, namely the exteriorising and articulating milieu of a signifying life open to communication. These general conditions must be disclosed not presumably by an inductive method for it would be an almost hopeless task, but by the consideration of hypotheses suggested by the study of the formal aspects of extant languages and by testing their capacity to resolve problems raised in the empirical analysis of languages. If a system of rules, to the extent that it is explicated, represents a meta-linguistic level with respect to the language it governs, then the general conditions which it must meet are situated, with respect to it, on the level of meta-theory.

If it belongs to linguistics to isolate the universal constituents of the structure of language, it falls to philosophic analysis to show how language can be meaningful. Of course in this area semantics paves the way; its task is to show by what mechanisms well formed sentences may be associated with a meaning. Still, while relying on the results of semantics, it remains necessary to examine the meaning relation as such, to distinguish its several dimensions and to understand its fundamental possibility. Semantics, too, has its philosophic side.

Once the generic nature of language has been worked out it remains to analyse its different uses. In this connexion we may usefully recall Wittgenstein's position in the *Philosophical*

Investigations: language does not function in a univocal way, but may be used in very diverse modalities. There is a multiplicity of 'language games'. Every different modality may be compared to a game which can be described by means of rules. This does not, however, entail arbitrariness. A 'language game' is a 'form of life' which means both that language is inseparable from a context (of situations, actions and interactions) and that it determines, by the particular form that it takes in a particular context, the peculiar quality characterising a certain form of experience. Accordingly the analysis of language, on condition that it is pushed beyond what pertains to the constitution of language as such, can be a privileged instrument allowing the differentiation of different regions of experience and the determination of what is proper to each. Rather than asking, for example, what opposes poetic to philosophic experience, one investigates the respective organisations of poetic and philosophic language. Into this context a study of the language of faith, its characteristic forms, its internal articulation, its particular way of structuring experience, fits quite easily.

One of the main problems emerging in such a study is the mode of signifying proper to the language of faith. It may be said that this language is not 'constative' (in Austin's sense), that it does not consist (at least in its absolute fundament) in speaking 'of' something, but that it is a form of language in which the speaker puts himself in question, operates on himself, causes a certain state of affairs in which he is implicated. Like all language it is meaningful, it articulates a certain area of meaning, it refers itself to a reality, but it does all this otherwise than does constative language. We have to examine what its internal structure can tell us about the proper modality of its signifying function. And in particular, we must ask if this structure can illuminate in any way the nature of the reality to which it refers. Does it disclose only the reality of the act itself, or also some other reality? If there is in fact a disclosure of some distinct reality, then it cannot be simply a language of

mere implication, cannot be reduced to being the expression
of an operation on the speaker himself. It must include a
constative element. But we must discover how and come to
understand in the language of faith this articulation of
auto- and hetero-reference, of implication and constation,
of relation to itself and relation to something else (viz.
salvation).

The analysis might be attempted from a number of
different perspectives. The place of experimental science
today and its importance suggests the perspective of the
following studies. The astonishing success of science, its
penetration in the domain of human phenomena (which is
today undeniable) its epistemological efficacy, its implications on the level of technological competence, has given it
the appearance of a privileged form of knowing. It has
provided us with a new image of the world which has
definitively replaced the archaic representations employed
by the various religions to formulate their interpretation of
the human—and even the divine—condition. It is not only
the vision of nature which has been profoundly modified
by science; man's vision of himself has been likewise changed.
Philosophy seems increasingly disqualified in favour of the
scientific forms of knowledge. At all events its proper sphere
seems to be continuously shrinking in face of the triumphal
extension of science. The idea is abroad that only scientific
knowledge is legitimate. And in neo-positivism we have a
philosophical school ready to assert that science alone is
capable of giving knowledge a content and that the task of
philosophy is meta-scientific: the study of how scientific
language functions. This view of science leads to a radical
reductionism: in principle it will be possible to account for
all aspects of human experience by scientific methods.
Formulated in terms of language, this enterprise appears as
a vast programme of transcribing all forms of language into
the privileged language of science. In particular the
language of faith is thought of as the formulation of a naïve
representation of reality still within the bonds of a mythic

mentality; the problem is to explicate this language and its correlative experience within the framework of an adequate scientific theory, for instance a purely operative conception of affectivity.

Even if one adopts a more liberal attitude and admits that there are forms of language non-reducible either directly or indirectly to scientific language, one may still consider that only the scientific method can furnish an acceptable world-view, for it alone allows for a strict control of the steps it prescribes, and that the non-scientific forms of language are to be considered only as expressions of subjectivity, utterly alien to the order of knowledge and consequently incapable of giving an objective structuring of reality. At the very least, one will be inclined to the view that the form of mind generated by scientific praxis is hardly compatible with the type of attitude implied by faith.

This situation calls for a confrontation between the two approaches. And, as has been already suggested, the analysis of language provides a good instrument for the task. In order to locate faith with respect to science it would seem more fruitful to compare the modes of functioning of their respective languages than to attempt to isolate and compare their respective 'essences'. As well as restoring to faith its proper meaning in the cultural context marked by the emergence of scientific reason, the comparison provides a way of approach to the language of faith that is not without certain advantages: by illuminating the specific traits of this language to the extent that they are distinguished from scientific language, the comparison throws light on the internal functioning of the language of faith. By showing how scientific language is related to the reality which it would describe and explain, it allows for a more precise idea of how the language of faith signifies, how it is to be distinguished from constative language, how it none the less includes a referential dimension that is not reducible to the mere effectuation of a self-involving act.

This perspective underlies the following essays. The first

and second are concerned with scientific language which may be divided into three domains: the language of the formal sciences, the language of the empirico-formal sciences, and the language of the hermeneutic sciences. The underlying problem is that of the prospective power of scientific language. Nowhere is this power merely a technique for description and classification. The essential moment is theoretic. But what is theory? Is it merely a convenient dodge allowing the connexion of some observable phenomena with other observable phenomena? Or has it some inventive productivity which allows it to run ahead of experience, to guide research, and to provide, finally, a representation which goes well beyond a mere synthesis of facts. The first essay approaches this question in a general fashion apropos of three separate groups of disciplines. The second essay introduces some precision on the subject of the formal sciences and the status of purely operative concepts.

There follows three essays on the interpretation of selected 'language games'. The first deals with the interpretation of scientific language in neo-positivism and its attitude to metaphysical propositions. The adequacy of the image of science proposed by the neo-positivists is questioned. The second essay examines the work of Donald D. Evans on self-involving language.[1] The theory of religious language elaborated by Evans from Austin's ideas opens up very interesting perspectives for the interpretation of the language of faith. Some difficulties remain, however. In particular it is at least questionable if a complete account of a self-involving language can be given without introducing 'constatives'. And if the language of faith, in one way or another, includes constative statements, there arises the problem of a criterion for their verification. In other words, the language of faith does not depend entirely on performative criteria (is the statement really operative, does it in

[1]The essay that appears in this translation is an amalgam of the essay here referred to and another, and shorter article by Professor Ladrière on the same topic. See Acknowledgements, p. 203–4—*translator's note*.

fact produce the effect that it connotes?) but on truth-criteria as well. But by what procedure can one assign to the statements of the language of faith their truth-value? This problem is inseparable from the problem of the meaning of the statements of faith. To know on what truth criteria they depend, one must know to what reality they refer (by their very structure). At this point, the hermeneutical problem arises. To ask how the language of faith signifies is to ask how it is to be interpreted. The interpretation has to appeal to certain speculative concepts. There are, for instance, cosmological and ethical interpretations. The question of the relation between the language of faith and cosmological language is broached in the final essay. The question of the relation between the language of faith and ethical language is only alluded to. However, the fifth essay does provide some contributions to its elucidation. For it is an analysis of the language of decision, a theme which introduces us to the domain of action, which is close to that of ethics. It concerns only a small point within the whole domain of action; still it may suggest lines of possible development.

In the last two essays we take up again the language of faith. Of these, the first resumes the path opened up at the beginning of the collection but this time a more elaborate attempt is made to disclose the connexions and distinctions between the languages of science, philosophy and faith. The last essay takes up the question of the incidence of cosmo-logical representations in the language of faith. It suggests a distinction between discourse and spoken word which would allow, at least as a first approximation, the location of the language of faith, interpreted here as 'spoken word', with respect to the different 'discourses' within which the manifold enterprise of reason is organised, and by which and in which it constructs itself at once as universal constituting power and as system.

All this is no more than a summary indication. The problem of faith's proper mode of meaning remains.

Definitions and Distinctions

IT may be useful here to bring together some definitions and distinctions relevant to the general context of linguistic analysis, which is that of these essays.

From the viewpoint of contemporary linguistics a *language* may be regarded as the (virtually infinite) set of well-formed sentences which can be generated by a determinate grammar, i.e., by a finite set of generative rules allowing the formation of complex units which make complete sense (sentences) by means of a number of elements (which may be abstract and are not in the general case directly reached on the level of perception). According to Chomsky a grammar has three components: syntactic, phonological and semantic. The syntactic component generates an abstract structure which has to be 'interpreted' by the two others. It produces and categorises units which function syntactically; in particular, syntactic units corresponding to sentences. The phonological component associates phonetic representations with these units and the semantic component associates them with meanings. Thus, by means of abstract structures, a grammar allows the association of significations with acoustically decipherable signals.[1]

The concept of language may be presented somewhat differently in terms of a cybernetic model as an ideal structure with a physical base (graphic, acoustic, electric, etc.) allowing the communication of information through a

[1]See N. Chomsky and G. Miller, *L'analyse formelle des langues naturelles*, Paris: Gauthier-Villars, La Haye, Mouton, 1968.

system of coding, transmission and decoding.[2]

Both views of language are within the objectivising perspective proper to science. The fruitfulness of this approach is shown in the event and is, as it were, imposed by the nature of language which presents itself as an objective structure. This is not to deny the legitimacy of a speculative approach to language which would regard it as a fundamental human possibility, an ontological modality.

It will be useful to distinguish *natural* and *artificial language*. The former is language as given, as spontaneously used by the members of different linguistic communities. Its rules operate implicitly and it falls to analysis to bring them to light. Artificial language is constructed and is language only in a derivative sense. Its rules are set down explicitly and completely and expressions are generated by the explicit (and voluntary) application of the rules. Consider for example the languages used in the formulation of formal systems. A formal language cannot, strictly speaking, be called a 'language' unless it includes rules of interpretation to allow the association of meanings with well-formed expressions. Less strictly, any process that allows the generation of expressions can be called a formal 'language' even when it is not accompanied by rules of interpretation, provided that at least some of the expressions so generated can be considered as 'sentences', i.e., as linguistic units susceptible (in a formal sense) of being 'true' or 'false'.

Within a formal language understood in this way one can construct a formal *system* by inventing a procedure to generate the class of 'true' sentences. If an interpretation can be associated with this language, then by means of semantic rules, one can specify which of the sentences are 'true'. (A 'normal' interpretation will place in the category of 'true' sentences all those which, in terms of that particular interpretation, represent an actual state of affairs.) A formal

[2]On this concept of language cf. L. Apostel 'Epistemologie de la linguistique' in *Logique et connaissance scientifique*, ed. Jean Piaget, Paris: Gallimard, 1967, 1056–96.

system may be regarded as a language; it is a process for the generation of a set of sentences.

In the study of languages, it is necessary to distinguish *language* and *meta-language*. For a given language L, the languages in which the properties of L are studied will be called meta-languages of L. L itself will be termed *object-language*. Three kinds of meta-language may be distinguished: syntactic meta-languages or *syntaxes*, *semantic*, and *pragmatic* meta-languages. Syntax studies the internal structure of the object-language. Its central concern is the elucidation of the workings of the generative rules and, in case the object-language either contains or constitutes a formal system, the workings of the deductive rules which generate the 'true' sentences of the system. Semantics studies signification, the relation between the terms in the object-language and their meaning. Pragmatics studies the conditions of actual usage of a given language.

It is difficult to characterise the notion of *signification*. All the terms of a language do not signify in the same way. We restrict ourselves to a few pointers.

Certain terms represent an entity (whether real or ideal) with which they have a relation of *reference* and which is called their *referent* (e.g. proper names, nominal clauses preceded by the definite article, abstract nouns). This relation can be defined by saying that an expression refers to an object if it can be used in a sentence to indicate that the sentence concerns this object.[3] For expressions which have a referent, signification can be considered as the referential relation.

For certain categories of expressions (among which some include and others exclude referents) the relation of signification can be analysed into two distinct relations: denotation and connotation. This is the case with nominal clauses, predicates and sentences. A nominal clause *denotes* or *names* a given non-linguistic entity: its referent. Besides this, the

[3]W. Alston, *Philosophy of Language*, Englewood Cliffs. N.J.: Prentice Hall, 1965, p. 15.

expression has a meaning and several expressions can have the same referent but different meanings. It may be said that it *expresses* or *connotes* its meaning. This meaning constitutes a concept (considered here as an abstract entity) which characterises or determines the referent. A predicate (or a complex predicative expression) *denotes* the class of objects to which it can be attributed and *connotes* a property (constituting a concept); it cannot be attributed to objects other than those which possess that property and which that property determines. The distinction between denotation and connotation with respect to predicates corresponds to the classical distinction between *extension* and *comprehension* (or *intension*). (Note that these latter terms are sometimes applied to concepts which are abstract objects or mental terms (depending on one's theory), rather than to predicates which are linguistic entities.)

The same distinction can be applied to sentences. In modern logic it is common to distinguish *sentences* and *propositions*. A sentence is a linguistic unit making complete sense, but considered solely from the syntactic point of view in abstraction from its signification. A proposition is an ideal entity and the semantic correlate of the sentence. For Frege, a sentence *denotes* or *names* truth value ('true' and 'false' being considered as abstract objects) and *connotes* or *signifies* a proposition. On this view, the sentence appears as a sort of nominal expression which has truth value as a referent and a proposition for meaning.

The terms *denotation* and *connotation* can be used to distinguish the objects with which a linguistic entity has a *relation* of denotation or connotation.

Certain linguistic terms have no signification in isolation; the syncategorematic expressions. This is indicative of the complexity of the relation of signification linking language to the domain spoken of. It is not the case that the various linguistic units are all in a one-to-one determinate semantic relation with extra-linguistic elements. This is the case for some only. One is thus inclined to think that the semantic functioning of a language should be considered as a global phenomenon rather than as a relation analysable into elementary relations.

Austin has developed the theory of signification as concerning sentences beyond the position that had become traditional since Frege. He distinguishes three dimensions of signification: locutionary, illocutionary and perlocutionary. The locutionary aspect of a sentence is its denotation and connotation (or meaning). The illocutionary aspect of a sentence is the specific form which makes the sentence a constative, an order, a promise, the expression of an attitude (of gratitude, confidence etc.), a verdict, an appreciation etc. According to Austin's theory, by uttering a sentence I *do* something, for instance I *affirm* a state of affairs, or I *make* a promise, or I *give* an order and so forth. The perlocutionary aspect is the effect the sentence produces in the listeners.

A language may be thought of as a system of signs of a particular kind. It may be said that a sign (considered as a material object) designates or represents another entity (which can be an ideal object or a concrete object—in the last analysis another sign). Pierce's distinction between three kinds of sign is well known: icons, indexes and symbols. An *icon* refers to the object which it denotes simply in virtue of its proper characteristics. An *index* refers to the object which it denotes in so far as it is really affected by this object. A *symbol* refers to the object it denotes in virtue of a rule the effect of which is to cause the symbol to be interpreted as referring to the object; the rule establishes an arbitrary link between symbol and object. Language falls under the category 'symbol', in Pierce's terms.

With reference to the distinction between *sentence* and *proposition* we may note that when a criterion of verification is applicable it may be said that a sentence is an expression susceptible of being true or false. Specifically, in the case of artificial languages, a sentence is to be defined thus (at least when the logic used is two-valued. More generally it may be said that a sentence is an expression susceptible of association with a truth-value). If one confines oneself to a formal language, leaving out of account the rules of interpretation (which give signification to its expressions), the terms 'true' and 'false' have merely formal and conventional sense: they are simply 'values' associated with certain expressions in conformity with certain prescriptions. (For example, one enumerates a list of 'true' sentences, the 'axioms' and deductive rules for the generation of 'true' sentences from 'true' sentences.) When a criterion of truth is not applicable (as is the case with performatives which are not 'constatives') one must specify a sentence as an expression capable of expressing its corresponding act (promise, verdict, etc.).

The status of a proposition has been the occasion of controversy. Some authors make propositions into platonic entities. Others, influenced by a nominalist epistemology, make them into classes of synonymous sentences. For Frege a proposition is an objective entity, neither a mental content nor a linguistic entity. Church takes up a position very near to Frege's when he defines a proposition as 'the meaning content which is common to the sentence and its translations in other languages'[4] or again as a concept which determines a truth-value.[5] A proposition, thus understood, is not a linguistic entity; it is obtained by abstraction from language. It seems possible to consider a proposition as the connotation (sense) of a sentence without recourse to the quasi-platonism of Frege, by relying on the suggestions of scientific semantics.[6]

The word *proposition* in an earlier sense meant the judgement in so far as it is expressed in words. In this sense the proposition is taken as a linguistic entity but in both its syntactic and its semantic dimensions: it is at once the sentence and its signification. Nevertheless in some contexts

[4]A. Church, 'Propositions and Sentences' in *The Problem of Universals*, Chicago: University of Notre Dame Press, 1956, 5.

[5]See A. Church, *Introduction to Mathematical Logic*, Princeton University Press, 1956, 26.

[6]On this issue see P. Gochet's: *Esquisse d'une theorie nominaliste de la proposition. Essai sur la philosophie de la logique* (Collection 'Philosophies pour l'âge de la science'), Paris 1972.

the term *proposition* may designate the syntactic aspect, the sentence, alone.

In the body of this work the term *sentence* will rarely be used and then only in the context of the discussions of formal systems. In general, the distinction sentence–proposition will not be used and the term *proposition* will be taken to signify both sentence and its content.

I

Signs and Concepts in Science

I. INTRODUCTION

The following pages are an examination of the role of signs and concepts in science. To this end it will be useful to suggest definitions of the two terms. A sign may be defined as an expression able to carry meaning and a concept as an ideal representation by means of which the mind grasps a part of the real or the ideal world (either an individual or a class) or as a property, either individual or relational, susceptible of being related to a real or ideal entity. We must attempt to discover the way in which signs and concepts operate in the different sciences.

We must examine in particular the role of theoretic concepts in the sciences. Have they a real function? Are they necessary? And if so, how do they operate? Beneath these questions we must probe more deeply in an effort to locate scientific language as a whole, at least as relating to a particular point of view, that of an examination of signs.

It is hardly feasible to propose so boldly the elaboration of a general theory of scientific language. Such a project might even be totally illusory. For within the boundaries of what is called science there are several very different groups of disciplines, and within these groups a more precise analysis would disclose subgroups. For present purposes we may be content with an extremely general and schematic distinction: formal sciences, empirico-formal sciences, hermeneutical sciences.

The formal sciences are mathematics and logic. They may

be spoken of in the singular as the science of formal systems, provided, of course, that one includes under the notion of 'formal system' both mathematical theories in the traditional sense and logical theories, as well as all the meta-theoretic considerations relating to these disciplines.

The empirico-formal sciences are those constructed on the model of physics. They pursue an empirically reachable reality but use in the analysis of that reality resources discovered in the formal sciences.

Finally, the hermeneutical sciences are the sciences of interpretation. Hermeneutics is the discipline concerned with the interpretations of signs in general and symbols in particular. Every interpretative venture intends to disclose a signification which is not immediately apparent. Signification is a relation between a sign and an entity belonging to either the real or the ideal world (individual, class, property or relation). (The ideal world is the world of objects that cannot be grasped empirically, such as mathematical objects or purely logical realities.) The hermeneutical sciences intend, in fact, human reality, in so far as this may be reached in the traces it leaves in nature, i.e. in actions and in works. The presence of meaning is attested to both in human action and in the works of man. Hermeneutic method must intervene as soon as we have to do with meanings.

2.   SIGNS AND CONCEPTS IN THE FORMAL SCIENCES

Consider the place of signs and concepts in the formal sciences. The term 'sign' has in this case an extremely limited meaning: the signs in question are quite simply symbols in the restricted sense. We are not dealing here with the symbols of hermeneutics (which are signs of double reference whose first sense intends analogically a second sense which does not emerge apart from this intention), but exclusively with logical or mathematical—that is, formal, symbols. A formal symbol is an elementary unit forming part of the vocabulary of a completely formalised artificial language—that is, a language defined purely syntactically by means of an explicit system of rules, abstract from all reference to intuitive signification of expressions in actual use.

The symbols (or the signs, since the terms are, in this case, equivalent) which obtain in formal languages serve simply as supports to the formal systems which may be formulated according to the rules of these languages. A formal system is an artificial language endowed with procedures permitting the classification of the sentences (generated with the language in question) into two classes: the class of *true* sentences and the class of *false* sentences. (A sentence is an expression which represents, in a formal language, an affirmation relating to a state of affairs, and as such is susceptible of being either true or false.) The case of deductive or axiomatic systems is particularly important. In such systems the procedures allowing the identification of true sentences are presented in the form of a set of axioms and deductive rules. Axioms are those sentences which are asserted to be true. The deductive rules permit the generation from true sentences, operating as premisses, of another true sentence, the consequence. By means of the deductive rules operating on the axioms one eventually obtains all the true sentences of the system. Mathematical theories can take the form of deductive systems.

Using a terminology borrowed from Curry, we can say that formal symbolism furnishes the *presentation* of formal systems. A formal system is a reality in the ideal order. In order to be able to speak of it, to communicate to ourselves something about it, we must make it graspable in an appropriate graphic expression. Formal symbols have no function other than making formal systems accessible in a determinate presentation, which will, of course, be wholly contingent and conventional. We must distinguish 'presentation', 'representation' and 'interpretation'. A *presentation* of a system is a set of symbols by means of which the system is formulated. A *representation* of a system is a set of entities about which the properties and relations expressed in the true sentences of the systems are affirmed. An *interpretation* of a system is a correspondence between the sentences of the system and utterances relating to a domain of determinate entities (utterances for which the criteria of verification are well established), such that all the true sentences of the system are associated with true utterances. (For example, consider a formal system expressing the relation of ordering. The statements of ordinary arithmetic can be made to correspond to the sentences of this system by associating with an elementary sentence of the type: 'The indeterminate object x is in relation r with the indeterminate object y' (where r symbolises the relation of ordering), the arithmetical statement 'The whole number a is smaller than the whole number b'. On the basis of such a correspondence all the true sentences of the theory of ordinal relation become true arithmetical statements.) As Curry says, a formal system should be considered as the abstraction from its presentations, its representations and its interpretations.

So much for signs. What of concepts? In one sense it may be said that there are no concepts in a purely formal system, i.e. in an entirely formalised system. But such a system is unusable if its meta-theory is not known. For the meta-theory of a formal system explains how the system functions, for example what type of deduction is allowed within it. Similarly, the meta-theory indicates the possible interpretations of the system and, accordingly, the meanings that are to be attached to the expressions of the system. In the meta-theoretic study of a system we must introduce concepts to represent the entities which are constitutive of the system (symbols, complex expressions, rules, deductive figures etc.) and the properties of these entities. Thus the non-contradictoriness of the system (the impossibility of deducing sentences arbitrarily within the system) is a meta-theoretic property; this property is represented by a meta-theoretic concept.

On the other hand, a formal system is of hardly any interest as long as it is not interpreted. Every interpretation of a system relates it to a certain domain of objects whether real or ideal. The statements relating to that domain are expressed by means of concepts. In the majority of cases for the formal systems studied so far, interpretations refer to logical or mathematical domains. The concepts employed to characterise these domains refer to ideal entities. Logic deals with discourse and the different forms of reasoning; mathematics with the ideal objects treated in the several departments of that discipline—numbers, sets, algebraic structures, spaces and so on.

The following problem arises with respect to concepts: are we to say that the concepts employed in the formal disciplines (whether we are dealing with meta-theoretic concepts or logical and mathematical concepts which are represented by the expressions of pure formal languages) have a merely descriptive role, or have they some explanatory power? It would appear that they can be allowed a certain measure of explanatory force. Thus the concepts of combinatory logic explain paradoxes, which are purely logical situations that can be represented in a formalism. The explanation consists of bringing into play another formalism that is foundational with respect to the former. (More exactly, the logical concepts employed can be represented in a formalism which clarifies the situation in which the paradoxes are produced.) Of course this explanatory formalism can in its turn produce situations generative of contradictions, like paradoxes. The analysis of these situations and the elimination of the source of difficulty demands a third theoretic level and so on.

There is no lack of examples to show the explicative role of concepts in mathematics. Thus the topological notion of dimension allows one to explain why there are not more points in a square than in one of its sides, in a cube than in a square. Here we are dealing with a situation which appears in the theory of transfinite cardinals. The situation is explained and the apparent paradox eliminated thanks to the concept of dimension and the corresponding theory.

Another example comes from the notion of group. This notion allows us to explain why the general equation of the fifth degree cannot be resolved by radicals. Here one is faced with an algebraic situation at a certain level which is clarified by more powerful algebraic concepts. The theory of groups gives the key to a structure of which the phenomenon to be explained is an exemplification.

The concepts of the formal sciences are, then, explanatory. But they explain by describing, as closer investigation reveals. Explanation is reached, in fact, by the invention of a more general structure. The concept is the means by which the mind grasps and characterises this structure. It does no more than describe the structure which affords the key to the situation to be explained. The concept in the formal sciences is then at once descriptive and explicative.

3. SIGNS AND CONCEPTS IN THE EMPIRICO-FORMAL SCIENCES

The empirico-formal sciences, to which we now turn, refer to empirical experience, but in their analyses of empirical reality they employ a theoretic apparatus which includes logico-mathematical instruments, i.e., instruments furnished by the formal sciences. Furthermore, this theoretic apparatus can be completely formalised.

In the general case there will be a purely mathematical dimension to the theories of the empirico-formal science, e.g., a geometry, infinitesimal analysis (or certain parts of it) and so on. But in these theories there will be also non-mathematical axioms of a specific kind, for instance the fundamental principle of dynamics (which expresses the proportionality between force and acceleration), or principles of variation or invariance. These axioms can be integrated into a formalised system in the same way as mathematical axioms. An empirico-formal theory can, accordingly, be expressed within a formal system which, as such, is not to be distinguished from a formal system representing a mathematical theory. But such a system cannot be reduced to its syntactical aspect. But even when an empirico-formal theory is expressed in a totally formalised way, the physical world is still intended through it; this intentionality will be represented at the level of scientific language by an appropriate interpretation which gives signification to the expression of the formalised theory; in other words, it endows the theory with its semantic dimension.

None the less, the situation is more complicated in the empirico-formal sciences than in the formal sciences for we must take into account both the empirical data and the manipulations (e.g. experimental manipulations) effected on them. Two sub-languages must, therefore, be introduced into empirico-formal language, namely, a theoretic language to express certain relations of general order between the entities and properties in terms of which one can analyse the reality to be studied, and an empirical language to describe the empirically observable aspects of this reality and the possible operations on it. The first language will contain non-logical terms: 'theoretic terms' which refer to entities or to properties among which some, most or all, may be non-observable. In this way one speaks of the electromagnetic field, inertial mass, spin, parity, etc. The second language too will contain non-logical terms, called 'empirical terms' referring to observable entities and properties. In this way one speaks of material bodies, galvanometers, length, weight, etc. Besides these terms both languages require linguistic and mathematical instruments such as ordinary logic, more or less extensive parts of mathematics (e.g. the theory of whole numbers, the theory of real numbers, of functions of real variables etc.). The theoretic language may be expected to contain more powerful logical and mathematical instruments than does the empirical language.

It is more accurate to say that these terms, whether theoretic or empirical, do not refer immediately to the objects or properties of which they speak. They correspond immediately to concepts (theoretic or empirical). More exactly, they *designate* concepts and the concepts *refer* to objects (whether real or ideal) or to the properties of objects.

Theoretic and empirical language must be put in relation to each other. To this end correspondence rules are introduced which allow the association of empirical terms with at least some of the theoretic terms. Thanks to these rules certain propositions from one language can be translated into the other. In many instances the correspondence rule associates a theoretic term with a measuring procedure; more exactly, it associates with the theoretic term an empirical term designating a property which is associated with a measuring procedure. (So the theoretic concept of temperature as it appears in thermodynamics can be made to correspond with the empirical concept of temperature defined as the property measured by means of a thermometer.)

An (empirico-formal) theory, in the proper sense of the word, is a set of propositions, formulated in a theoretic language, which are taken as axioms, and a set of propositions expressing the correspondence rules. (If the theory is entirely formalised we should speak of 'sentences' rather than of 'propositions'. A sentence is a linguistic entity which can represent a proposition. A proposition is an ideal entity consisting of a grasp of a state of affairs. Here we ignore this distinction and speak simply of 'propositions'.) The propositions which have been taken as axioms are considered as, at least provisionally, true. They play the role of hypotheses. By means of the introduction of the deductive rules accepted within the theory, other propositions may be deduced which are the *theorems* of the theory. As for the correspondence rules, since they necessarily involve theoretic terms, they must be considered as part of the theory and are also hypothetical.

It is possible for us at this point to indicate the nature of explanation in the empirico-formal sciences. In these sciences, explanation is essentially a deduction from the axioms of the theory of propositions which thanks to correspondence rules can be translated into propositions of the empirical language and so is directly testable by observation. Note, however, that every explanation presupposes some information relating to the reality in question, namely *initial conditions*. The total process of explanation appears to be as follows. One observes the state of the system to be studied at a determinate instant; in other words, the initial conditions of the problem are given. These conditions are expressed in an empirical proposition the content of which is introduced into the theoretic language, thanks to the correspondence rules, as a theoretic proposition. This proposition, linked with the axioms of the theory, allow, thanks to the deductive rules, a new proposition which is translatable into the empirical language as a proposition expressing a certain state of affairs relating to the system at a given instant (a later instant than that of the initial conditions). If that state of affairs is in fact the one observed at that instant, then one has reached an explanation. It would seem that explanation consists in establishing a link between antecedent and consequent by means of a logical structure of a theoretic order. The predictive process obeys the same schema from the logical viewpoint.

Explanation, as it has just been described, concerns the evolution of a system in time. There are other kinds of explanation, for instance the explanation of a configuration by means of conditions expressing limits. Still, explanation by antecedents furnishes the most representative case of the explicative process and throws into relief what is essential in all forms of explanation, namely the introduction of a deductive movement.

The problem concerning the role of concepts in the empirico-formal sciences can now be stated accurately. The question is whether or not theoretic concepts have an essential function? Could they, in principle, be eliminated? At this juncture it is necessary to recall two very important logical facts: on the one hand, the formulation of theoretic propositions in the form of 'Ramsey sentences', and, on the other hand, Craig's theorem.

Consider Ramsey sentences. Take, to simplify matters, a theory with only two theoretic terms T_1 and T_2. Make a conjunction of all the propositions constituting the axioms of the theory. In the proposition thus obtained, replace the terms T_1 and T_2, whenever they appear, by variables, x and y, and introduce existential quantities for these variables. We get a sentence of the form: 'There exists an indeterminate x and an indeterminate y such that, between them, the following relations hold . . .' (that is, the relations expressed in the axioms of the theory). This sentence is the Ramsey sentence for the theory and it can be shown to permit precisely those deductions allowed by the theory itself. As regards its explanatory and predictive power it is equivalent to the initial theory. The Ramsey sentence for any theory must be considered as having the same empirical content as that theory. But if one has recourse to this formulation it is no longer necessary to suppose the existence of the non-perceptible entities and their properties referred to in the theory. Accordingly, recourse to Ramsey sentences allows for the elimination of theoretic concepts from scientific language.

We come now to Craig's theorem. Let there be a series of propositions constituting an explanation in the sense described above. This series must include an empirical proposition that describes the situation at a given instant, considered as the initial instant, a certain number of theoretic propositions that purport to furnish an explanation, intermediary propositions, and an empirical proposition that describes the situation of the system at a certain instant distinct from the initial instant. Intermediary propositions are chains of derivation leading from the empirical proposition which describes the initial state through explicative propositions to the empirical proposition which describes the state to be explained. They contain at once theoretic and empirical terms. Very schematically, Craig's theorem shows that this series of propositions can be replaced by another which is devoid of theoretic terms and which, therefore, links the proposition expressing the initial state with the proposition expressing the state to be explained by a chain of propositions which include only empirical terms. Accordingly, theoretic terms can be completely eliminated in the explanatory process.

On the showing of these logical results, theories have no more than an inessential and artificial character. Basing their opinion on these conclusions, radical empiricists hold that a theory is no more than a convenient presentational instrument, in Quine's neat phrase 'a useful device'. Is this a correct interpretation of the role of theory? The proposed 'reductions' have something artificial about them. In the case of Ramsey sentences the problem is merely displaced. Although they seem to suppress the question of the status of 'theoretic' entities, in fact they reintroduce the question in a new guise: 'ontological presuppositions'. What entities must be presupposed (at least implicitly) to exist if a proposition with existential quantifiers is to be considered meaningful? In the case of Craig's theorem we have a procedure permitting the elimination of theoretic terms from a given explanatory derivation, but we have no general procedure which allows explanation without recourse to theoretic term. The permitted 'reduction' is valid only for particular explanations: given a determinate explanation one can reformulate it using only empirical terms.

But a theory is not a set of particular explanations. It does not limit itself to explaining a collection of known facts nor to predicting facts belonging to a class of already known facts. The purpose of a theory is to make known to us a certain domain of reality. Empirical experience is introduced only as a check on theory. The history of science shows that theory has a prospective role. The content of a theory is not to be reduced to the sum of experiments already carried out which confirm it, nor even to the sum of possible confirmatory experiments belonging to a determinate class. The content of the theory is extended presumptively to cover regions still unexplored: theory is intended to facilitate the discovery of new facts, if possible facts that belong to an as yet unknown class.

The reductionist position just outlined is linked to a strictly inductionist viewpoint. On this view, theories express what is already known and are progressively confirmed by the accumulation of facts. But this way of seeing things does not at all correspond to the real status of the theories discoverable throughout the history of science—particularly theories of great significance. These theories are interpretative contexts in principle capable of resisting being put to the test, that is, they set themselves up as covering the entire domain under investigation. Their validity is, of course, only provisional: they are eliminated and replaced by others as soon as they fail one of the tests to which they are subjected.

There is, then, an anticipatory character in theory; its role is to allow or organise experience in advance. If this is the case we must recognise that it has real fecundity being at once explicative and prospective. It remains to be seen how we can account for this fecundity. We may suggest two reasons for it. On the one hand, the theory has recourse, as we have seen, to the resources of formal systems, that is to the resources of operational thought, which carries a privileged intelligibility, for it makes no appeal to intuition, whether intellectual or empirical. It understands in effecting what is to be understood. For instance, we understand the meaning of the notion of group by operating with the axioms which define this notion and by discovering through deduction what the axioms contain. The meaning of a system of rules is understood by seeing how the system functions. On the other hand, we may note that in the last analysis a theory is no more than the formalisation of an anticipatory intention, of a fore-understanding of the domain. Formalisation gives a precise content to this fore-understanding and at the same time gives it operative status. This fore-understanding remains present in the operations which express it and so it goes beyond the mere grasp of a determinate collection of facts, it goes beyond the already known, it envisages the horizon within which all facts of a certain category are situated, namely, a style of presence and operation. If the theory expresses operatively the prevailing vision which underlies its movement, it is not surprising that it has prospective power.

What of signs? As an approach to this question we must examine the role of experiments in the empirico-formal sciences. In the strict sense an experiment is a process by which one attempts, by varying the circumstances in a controlled fashion, to determine the function of this or that variable which is in principle isolable. An experiment leads to observations whose results are expressed in empirical propositions: observational propositions. For strict empiricism these propositions directly express a datum. This datum is a content of perception and is considered as the ultimate instance of scientific truth. The reductionist viewpoint considered above is linked with this empiricism. The point of the reductive processes is to confine scientific language in the end to observational propositions. On this view the meaning of empirical propositions accrues to them wholly from perception. Meaning is translated from empirical to theoretic propositions; the latter being introduced simply as a convenience of language.

It would seem that this conception is open to criticism. In reality, observational propositions do not express the observed datum so much as the manner in which the datum of perception is interpreted. Every interpretation relates unavoidably to a conceptual interpretative framework, i.e. to a theory. There is no way of expressing in a proposition a content given in perception without using an interpretative instrument which is necessarily theoretic. Feyerabend has offered a logical demonstration of this fact.[1] Let there be a phenomenon *P*, an event in the world perceived by us. And let the proposition *S* express this phenomenon. From the viewpoint of strict empiricism it is supposed that the signifi-

[1] See 'Problems of Empiricism', in Robert G. Colodny (ed.), *Beyond the Edge of Certainty*, Englewood Cliffs, N.J.: Prentice Hall, 1965, 145–260.

cation of this proposition is adequately and uniquely determined by the phenomenon P. We may ask how it happens that the proposition S is adequate to the phenomenon P which it expresses, and how this adequation is known. If one takes up a strictly empiricist position there can be no thought of accounting for this adequation in other than phenomenal terms. One must, accordingly, introduce a second phenomenon R indicating that the proposition S is adequate to the phenomenon P. But how is one to be sure that the phenomenon R is pertinent, that it is adequate to the situation—that is, that it is effectively capable of showing that the proposition S is adequate to the phenomenon P? If one would remain faithful to the strictly empiricist viewpoint it is necessary to introduce a third phenomenon T expressing the pertinence of R. And so one is caught in a 'regressus ad infinitum'.

From this Feyerabend concludes that the strictly empiricist theory of observational propositions must be abandoned. In its stead he proposes a pragmatic theory of observation. Doubtless observational and theoretic propositions must be distinguished. But observational propositions are distinct not because they are the adequate expression of a content of perception but because of the circumstances of their production. What differentiates observational from theoretic propositions is the nature of the operative context within which they are elaborated. The foundational hypothesis of Feyerabend's epistemology is that there exists a real objective world which contains the observer and which is such that between our sensations and the events of the world there is a high degree of correlation. Sensations and perceptions are simply indicators. They play a role wholly analogous to that of instruments. Just as the result furnished by an instrument has to be interpreted, so our sensations and perceptions have to be interpreted. Observational propositions which correspond to them are in reality interpretations. Every interpretation presupposes criteria and among those chosen for observational propositions will be this one in particular: the interpretation adopted must make it impossible to hold a proposition of fact indefinitely. This comes down to saying that no observational proposition can be regarded as ultimate and unrevisable. According to the pragmatic theory of observation there is no irreducible observational kernel.

If this is the case, then we are faced with a circle which we may call the methodological circle of the empirico-formal sciences. With respect to the domain studied and subjected to observation, the theory is an *a priori*. It is not the result of an induction. It is a logical structure which is provisionally constituted as valid and which must be put to the test. The structure is governed by extremely general principles (as the principles of conservation or the variational principles in physical theories) whose validity is accepted in the name of a kind of rational belief in the intelligibility of world. These principles in their content express a pre-comprehension of the domain studied, founded on a familiarity with the domain, but at the same time going beyond what is already known of it. This throws us back to a moment of gift, an underlying meeting between scientific subject and world. On the other hand, the choice of a particular formalism imposes, *ipso facto*, a particular way of approaching the object, mediated by correspondence rules which indicate how we can associate a theoretic interpretation with observation propositions and which allow at the same time the elaboration of experimental procedures. In this way the object is attained through an interpretative instrument.

There is, accordingly, a circle: the construction of theories presupposes a fore-understanding of the object and therefore an original *gift*, but on the other hand, the object is not given except through the medium of an interpretation. This circle is historical: one moves from more elementary to more elaborate theories. But basically one never escapes from language and language has a theoretical aspect. None the less, the movement from fore-understanding to formalised theory is not useless, for formalisation adds to fore-understanding the intelligibility of the operation; thus the fore-understanding attains an articulation and a clarity which it would not otherwise have.

In one sense we might say that the empirico-formal strategy is a decoding of signs. If observation has the role of indicator, theory must be compared to a resonator. We have no other means of understanding reality than by re-inventing it. We cannot know in advance if our chosen interpretative instrument is appropriate. Theory represents merely a possible world. To know the real world—which is the object of the exercise—we have to introduce the empirical moment in the process, i.e. the theory must be subjected to test. But we can observe only a tiny part of the immense ocean of facts; we touch the continuum of reality only at a few points. Our effort is to discover if there is a resonance between reality and our conceptual apparatus. If we can *affirm* such resonance we have some justification for considering our theory correct, at least for a certain domain. But all this is never more than a presumption. In any case, the theory is not an image of the world, but rather a conjectural reconstruction of reality.

This can be illustrated in the particularly striking case of probablist theories. For all variables under consideration these theories yield not determinate values but only distributions of probabilities. What do probabilities represent? Some authors have considered them to be properties of the variables to which they refer—a position which leads into considerable difficulties. It would seem that these probabilities should be represented as purely ideal elements somewhat like the points to infinity in a geometry. We construct an ideal, abstract space, the space of possibilities (relative to a given property), for instance the space of the possible values of a physical variable (which at any instant has in itself a fully determinate value).[2] To each of these possibilities we

[2]This is Popper's view. See 'Quantum Mechanics Without "The Observer"', in Mario Bunge (ed.), *Quantum Theory & Reality*, Berlin—Heidelberg—New York: Springer Verlag, 1967, 7–11.

assign a certain weight, in the form of a probability. We then make conjectures about the form of distribution of these weights or the temporal evolution of the distribution. Indirectly, therefore, we give indications concerning the real value to be expected. A probabalist theory constitutes a picture which enables us to interrogate reality or to make an image of reality. The way in which the reality responds leads us eventually to change our description of the space of possibilities, to employ another type of distribution. But we remain always in conjecture.

4. SIGNS AND CONCEPTS IN THE HERMENEUTICAL SCIENCES

Finally we turn to the examination of the status of signs and concepts in the hermeneutical sciences, by which are meant in the first place those which are also called the human sciences. These sciences are dominated by a great debate as to whether they should model themselves on the natural sciences or consider themselves to be in a special position which demands other methods. Are they reducible or not to the natural sciences, i.e. the empirico-formal sciences? There are cases when reduction to quantified description—in statistical form in the long run—or to algebraic description is possible. In demography, for instance, the statistical viewpoint is fruitful, and, as structuralism has shown, in the study of cultures algebraic notions have been useful in dealing with some problems. Yet it seems that there are domains in which meaning plays a role that is not to be eliminated, for example, in the study of documents or of political action. The problem is this: how to study scientifically—that is from the standpoint of professedly critical knowledge—phenomena which include meanings. A meaning is never given in apodictic evidence of an intuitive type; it is accessible only through its traces—works, actions, institutions.

These indices through which we are given meanings are

signs—that is, referential realities referring to a sense in itself invisible. In the domains under consideration the sign itself becomes the object of study. It comes in not merely as the sign of something else but as a reality to be studied on its own account. None the less, the sign must always be considered as what it essentially is, namely as the carrier of a meaning. The meaning may be twofold to make the problem even more complex. For if one meaning is superimposed on the other, how are you to move through the first to the second? When the meanings are detachable from one another the answer is easy, as in allegory where the relation between first and second meaning is contingent and external. The second meaning may be expressed differently; in other words, translation is enough to highlight the second meaning with complete clarity, but the problem is very much more difficult when the second meaning cannot be detached from the first, when it is accessible only through the first, as in the case of symbol.

We can get a more accurate picture of the situation of the hermeneutical sciences if we consider briefly some typical cases. First, history. The problem is to reconstitute past events from present documents and to reach an understanding of these events. This can be broken down into two sub-problems: first, there is the move from documents to events and secondly, there is the explanation of these events. The first sub-problem evokes a theory of objectification. We have to understand how the intentions and actions of the actors are projected into external signs whose trace remains, how they can be set down in objectifications that are transmissible over time. If we can succeed in working out a theory of this kind, then we have at our disposal an instrument which will allow us to move back from signs to actions and intentions, so from events to their meaning.

As for the second sub-problem, explanation, it raises other theoretical difficulties. Two types of explanation may be put forward: explanation in terms of projects or explanation in terms of systems. In the one case, the projects formed or lived by the actors are the centre of attention. In the other, attention is directed to totalities, global configurations, which envelop many actions and in which the contribution of the individual actor is ignored. An explanation in terms of projects demands the elaboration of a theory analysing the possible links between situations and projects, and, relying on the theory and as a function of known situations, one must work out types of possible projects to act as hypotheses in the explanatory process. Explanation in terms of systems, on the other hand, demands a theory about the evolution of systems. Here one might be influenced by theories of physical or biological systems (using a cybernetic model for instance); or one might rely on philosophical (accordingly, non-scientific) theories—e.g. a dialectical philosophy.

Have these strategies any validity? After all, the historian is himself implicated in his instrument of interpretation. One cannot abstract from the role played by the historic situation of the historian in the elaboration of his explanatory system. An adequate validation of the strategies of historical science would suppose a clarification of the historian's situation. If one's explanation is in terms of project, it is necessary to be able to wholly elucidate the nature of the project. Total reflexion must be possible. But is it? Is there not in every project an implicit aspect which cannot be captured in reflexion? Must we not likewise take account of unconscious motivations which escape reflexion, which are accessible only to such hermeneutical interpretation as is found in psychoanalysis (to which we return later)? On the other hand, in an explanation in terms of systems, one must, when the explanation is based on a physical theory, be able to reduce the explanation completely to physical terms, e.g. to an explanation of cybernetic type, or, when the explanation is based on a philosophy, one must be able to furnish a complete justification of that philosophy and of its role.

In neither case can the historical theory be its own foundation. To justify it one must introduce another kind of discourse. Two other types of justification are available: either metatheoretic or reliance on a pragmatic criterion. One may attempt to leave to the historian's discourse its own specificity and to justify it by means of a meta-theory which would be capable of considering the historian's situation from the outside. However the meta-theory will either be formalised or not; if it is, then we have once again another type of discourse. If it is not, then we have a physical or a philosophical theory, or else we have a theory which is open to exactly the same problems as the original historical theory itself. Or one may appeal to a pragmatic criterion. For instance, one might claim that the adequate viewpoint or the one that has to be regarded as justified, is whatever viewpoint is most progressive. This point of view will be defined as the one capable of expressing the totality. However, this too presupposes a philosophy which holds that there exists at any one time a viewpoint of the totality and that this viewpoint can be made explicit and described in an appropriate discourse. Once again we are forced to invoke a discourse of another type. In sum, whatever path we take we are always led back to another level. The problem of the justification of the historical hermeneutic becomes then the problem of reduction to a physicalist discourse, or the problem of the foundation of a philosophic discourse, or the problem of the foundational import of a formal meta-theoretic discourse.

Economic theory can serve as our second example. We have to analyse action in so far as it establishes a rational link between means and ends in a partially random situational context which includes the intervention of other actors whose ends are, partially or totally, opaque.

A particularly clear case of economic theory is games theory where the concept of strategy is central. A strategy is a space of possible ways of action which are weighted differently as a function of situation, of the constraints of the game and of the reactions of the other players in so far as these are known or conjectured. Recourse to a theory of this kind presupposes that behaviour is completely analysable in operative terms. The aim is to reach an entirely formalised representation of action. No matter how this representation is constructed, problems inevitably arise as soon as the theoretic schemas are applied to real situations, for example (as in games theory) to political and economic competition. As soon as one comes back to actual behaviour the situation is complicated by the intrusion of problems from psychology and sociology. Psychology demonstrates that motives are not to be restricted to conscious contents and that, consequently, the explanation of behaviour is not to be sought solely within the schemas of rational action. Sociology, for its part, has shown that the principles invoked in actual ways of acting, however apparently rational, depend on the particular conditions of the society in which the actors operate, and that these conditions are neither entirely explicit nor wholly rational.

A brief mention of psychoanalysis is called for. From this viewpoint behaviour is not to be entirely explained by conscious data; to account satisfactorily for behaviour it is essential to introduce an interpretation based on a theory of the unconscious. Since the unconscious is by definition inaccessible to a direct grasp, the mediation of a theoretic structure is required. One may ask how this structure justifies itself, taking into account its content—that is, what it affirms of the underlying motivations of discourse. Either it must be capable of issuing a complete elucidation of its own presuppositions, or else it must show itself independent of the unconscious. In the first case, it must be shown that complete control of the unconscious is possible, in other words a total reflexion of the unconscious within consciousness—a fairly ambitious undertaking. In the second case, it must be effectively demonstrated that psycho-analytic discourse is itself independent of the unconscious. This can be done by a physicalist reduction: psychoanalytic discourse will henceforth be regarded as a provisional formulation which leads eventually to an exhaustive interpretation of behaviour in physical terms, for instance in terms of cybernetics. It can be done also by a rigorous formalisation of the psychoanalytic discourse (as the structuralist interpretation of psychoanalysis seems to suggest). The discourse will not necessarily be physicalist but will have the same logical form as physical theories. Finally it can be done by an appeal to philosophy: in this case either psychoanalytic discourse will be treated as a variety of philosophic discourse, or a philosophic theory will be invented to serve as a foundation for psychoanalysis. Whatever method is adopted it must be shown how and why the interpretation selected (physicalist, formalist or philosophic) is privileged— that is, how it may be considered totally autonomous with respect to unconscious determinations in particular, or with respect to all extrinsic determination in general.

Linguistics is our final example. Linguistics uses the model suggested by information theory, which analyses the exchange of messages in terms of coding, transmission and decoding. It explains not only the finite aspects of language —i.e. the development and functioning of linguistic units which can be collected and catalogued at a given instant, but also the infinitistic aspects of language—i.e. the creative capacity of language which generates on the basis of a finite apparatus a discourse which is, in principle, indefinitely variable. It has provided a method for discovering the underlying rules which generate novel complex entities from a finite set of elementary entities, and has thus shown that besides the obvious structures of language there are deep structures which are accessible only to theoretical analysis. We have, then, a formal theory which explicates the immanent logic of language. This theory succeeds in objectifying completely the phenomenon under discussion; no place is left for a hermeneutic stage. There remains, however, the problem of restoring language to the speaking subject, or co-ordinating the structures with the vital intentionality which animates discourse. It must not be forgotten that language serves to evoke states of affairs and to communicate, that it is not merely a set of structures operating, so to speak, in a void or on their own account.

These examples introduce the fundamental problem of hermeneutics: the 'hermeneutic circle'. This may be simply stated: in the hermeneutic domain there is an identity between subject and object. The object cannot be apprehended except by means of instruments of understanding furnished by the subject, while the way in which the subject elaborates these instruments is itself determined by the situation as a whole; and it is precisely this situation which is the object of investigation. The 'hermeneutic circle' is shown in another way: the knowledge which one acquires of the object modifies both the object and—consequently—the interpreting subject. This is merely a variant of the fundamental problem.

The problem arises because the human object inescapably includes conscious states (in the broadest sense). Since these are invisible they cannot be attained except by an effort of comprehension. 'Comprehension' can be understood in two ways: it can designate either a mode of affective participation or a hypothetical reconstitution. Serious and apparently legitimate objections have been brought against the theory of affective participation: it leads perforce to a relativism and a subjectivism and cannot furnish objectivisable criteria. If this mode of comprehension is abandoned in favour of hypothetical reconstitution, adequate principles of interpretation must be set out. And the elaboration of such principles necessarily involves the interpreting subject and his comprehension of himself. This can be reformulated: every hermeneutical comprehension of another's behaviour is at the same time, and irredeemably, a self-comprehension of the interpreting subject.

Is there a difference between the hermeneutic circle and the methodological circle of the empirico-formal sciences? It would seem so, for hermeneutic fore-understanding does not aim at only an operative schema like that of the empirico-formal sciences; it aims at subjectivity and its intentionalities, an intentional dynamism. The real problem is to work out how this fore-understanding could be critical. As a general rule, the subject is either wholly or at least partially ignorant of his own principles of interpretation or at least of their ultimate presuppositions. The problem of a critical foundation for hermeneutics in as much as hermeneutics always includes self-comprehension is, accordingly, the problem of the self-elucidation of the interpreting subject. Not only must the subject become aware of the presuppositions operative in his interpretations, but he must also discover the criteria which will allow him to select adequate principles of interpretation and be able to furnish reasons for the supposed validity of the selected criteria. What is needed is a privileged interpretative situation or, to speak in terms of a language, the problem of a privileged language.

Is there a privileged language? And if so what is it? Are we to say that the language of physics serves as the foundation for all the others and allows us egress from the heremeneutic circle? But to affirm this is to introduce a presupposition stating that empirico-formal language is completely autonomous and in the last analysis able to found all other languages. Now this presupposition itself has to be expressed either in physicalist terms or in some other language. In the first case justification will fail—except by *petitio principii*. For it is not possible to justify in physicalist terms the extension of physicalist language to human phenomena without presupposing precisely that which has to be justified, namely the legitimacy of this extension. The second case involves one in contradiction: if the justificiatory discourse is not physicalist, then what one hoped to found is, in fact, abolished, namely the absolute autonomy of empirico-formal discourse.

Perhaps one will invoke a philosophic language as the privileged one. And once again one is faced with the daunting problem of the self-founding character of philosophy. How is such self-founding to be conceived? Should this take the form of a total reflexion, or, as strict empiricism suggests, should it rest on an ultimate given to which everything can be reduced? And is philosophy not itself a hermeneutic? Have we not to admit that all the problems of hermeneutic discourse are also problems of the philosophic discourse to which we would have recourse in our attempt to found hermeneutics? Conversely, on the hypothesis of a philosophic foundation, how are we to account for the autonomy of scientific discourse? For it seems difficult not to admit that contemporary science has constituted itself in total independence of philosophy.

5. CONCLUSION

The foregoing considerations prompt us to ask if the problem of the legitimation whether of hermeneutics or of formal and of empirico-formal sciences is well posed, if it is itself legitimate. The very fact of raising the problem presupposes that our efforts require ultimate justification, foundation— even self-foundation. Now this presupposition cannot be admitted without examination. Consider the different formulations of the problem of foundations throughout history. We discover that everywhere the problematic of foundations has shown limitations which raise doubts as to its well-foundedness.

In the formal sciences the foundational enterprise takes a strictly formalist guise: to found is to axiomatise and to furnish a demonstration of non-contradiction for the formalism so constituted. The enterprise has met with difficulties that have obliged logicians to recognise that a radical foundational programme is an impossible task. There exists no ultimate formal system capable of founding all others including itself (in the sense of a formalist theory of foundation).

In the empirico-formal sciences the idea of foundation has been most clearly formulated by the empiricists in the form of an ultimate reduction of all scientific propositions, including theoretic propositions, to propositions which are thought to express a pure given. But as we have seen, the viewpoint and reductionist programme of strict empiricism fails before both logical and empirical obstacles. There is a methodological circle in the empirico-formal sciences. There can be no appeal to an ultimate given. There are no protocol propositions as was hoped in the early days of neo-positivism. All propositions, even observational propositions, have a theoretic character; all propositions must be considered open in regard to ulterior verification. If there is no ultimate given, then (at least in the empiricist sense) there is no ultimate foundation.

As for the hermeneutical sciences, the question is the existence of a privileged language—that is, a form of language in which a complete self-elucidation of the interpreting subject can be achieved. The question may be precisely formulated thus: can hermeneutic discourse be reduced either to the discourse of physics or to philosophic discourse? We have seen the problems that arise in either case.

We are led to the idea of a knowledge that would be critical without being founded. It is perhaps illusory to consider the idea of justification in terms of an ultimate foundational discourse which is entirely apodictic. But the problem of justification remains. We must attempt to elucidate, at least partially, the presuppositions with which we operate. We must also demonstrate the fecundity of our methods, for the true justification of a method is its fecundity. But how is this to be defined? We can say that a method is fecund in so far as it is able to elicit understanding of the reality which we question. But what is understanding? There are several discourses, sciences and meta-sciences indicative perhaps of several modes of understanding. None the less, in every discourse, both theoretic and meta-theoretic, as in every effort at foundation and justification, there is one idea which is both unificatory and revelatory, namely the idea of truth.

There is a circularity about truth which is at the root of

the other circles, particularly of the hermeneutic and empirico-formal circles. The question concerning truth is one which presupposes itself. We already know what truth is as soon as we undertake the effort to know; the idea of truth is our guide. None the less, its presuppositions cannot be wholly elucidated since for us truth is not accessible in the form of a pure given, nor is there an already achieved truth in the form of an *a priori* construction. Truth is always to be made; it precedes and proclaims itself at the same time. It illuminates us but remains itself enigmatic. If there are many discourses, then philosophy is not privileged though it has its own proper task. It must become that discourse in whose context the problematic being of truth can show itself and in which the effort to understand can begin to understand itself—an endless task.

Finally, this position on the problematic and pluralist situation of science must itself be interpreted as a sign. It is indicative of the situation of human reason in general which is itself a question. We are measured by truth but we do not succeed in fully expressing its demands. We exist at once in clarity and in enigma. Reason has an intrinsic norm, an intentionality towards unity and transparence but can neither totally fulfil nor explicate itself. Yet it is lucid enough to recognise its limitation. A limit appears only against a non-limited background; it must therefore be seen not as a term marking the end of the course but as the trace of a finitude which carries within itself the acknowledgement of its impotence and the daring of a hope that is open to infinity.

II

Symbolism as Domain of Operations

I. INTRODUCTION

The purpose of this study is to show the significance of symbolism in the formal sciences and, in particular, to underline the place of the notion of operation in these sciences. The examination of this notion raises a question both epistemological and ontological: how is the efficacy of the operation to be explained and founded?

At first sight it seems unacceptable to talk of symbolism when dealing with the manipulations of the formal sciences since the problems that are studied in these sciences are far removed from the preoccupations of those who investigate the nature and significance of symbolism. Can we speak of symbols in the strict sense when dealing with a formal language? In the ordinary notion of symbol there is a significatory power which engages affectivity, rooted in the subterranean regions where belief, evidence and truth find their source. The symbol differs from the sign. If it refers us to something other than itself, it does not do so in the anonymous and conventional way of the sign, but as a function of its constitutive structure, because of a dynamism in itself, because in it meaning is, as it were, carried up and beyond itself. At first sight the symbols used in formal languages are simply indicators, empty places for an absent object, abstract instruments, distinct from their meaning. Yet here too there is a movement of going beyond, of breaking across barriers, towards a domain which remains strictly inexpressible, at least if one is limited to the expressions furnished by everyday language based on perception.

Furthermore, structuralist thought has established a relation between these two kinds of symbolic thought, poetic symbolic thought and formal symbolic thought. It has demonstrated that the key to myths, rites and indeed social relations—which both symbolise and are symbolised by myths—is structure. Now structure cannot be thought except in the framework of formal thought. Naturally one must take account of the support, the material in which the structure is embodied, but its function is subordinate and secondary. The devaluation of the notion of history shows this very clearly: structure is opposed to event, the intelligibility of the relation to the pure contingency of fact whose sole virtue is to be an occasion for the manifestation of structure. A well known theory of myth suggests that the function of myth is to bring us back to a primordial event, to an originating time outside and preceding ours, but capable of eternal rejuvenation. Structuralist thought destroys this interpretation. The structure is eternal. Reality is incessantly transformed but its transformations obey laws that are themselves structural so that, in the end, immobility dominates. Everything is given once for all. Nothing is essentially new in the parade of phenomena. Everything can be foreseen, everything is precontained in the wisdom of numbers and relations. To understand the reality of symbol in all its facets we must examine formal thought. This can be done in stages.

2. THE SYMBOL AS AN INSTRUMENT OF DESIGNATION

In the first place the symbol is abbreviated notation. As such, when it merely replaces more or less complex expressions of current language, it serves to reduce the volume of writing. At this level symbols represent the conventions of language and writing and have no intrinsic interest.

None the less, recourse to symbolic scripts begins to be

required as soon as there is question of representing ideal objects. Consider the numerals used to designate successive whole numbers. At first sight it would seem possible to name the latter using the words of ordinary language; the symbolism brings in nothing new. There is, however, in the series of whole numbers a peculiar property expressed in the phrase 'and so on'. How is one to represent an inexhaustible domain of individual elements by means of regulated procedures and without undue complexity?

This problem is resolved in two moves: the use of a base and the convention of position. Ordinarily the base 10 is used but this is arbitrary. The base 2 will do equally well and in this case all the whole numbers can be represented using only two symbols: 0 and 1. A particular number will be represented by means of a (finite) sum of terms which are multiples of successive powers of the base. The ordinary way of writing the numbers retains only the coefficients and the position of the numeral corresponds to the power of the base of which it is the coefficient. The number 327 will be represented on the base 10 by the following expression: $3.10^2 + 2.10^1 + 7.10^0$. The ordinary notation, 327, retains only the coefficients of this representation in their proper order. These coefficients are simply the remainders of successive divisions by 10 operated on the number 327. (Divide 327 by 10 to get 32 and 7 as a remainder; divide 32 by 10 to get 3 and 2 as a remainder; divide 3 by 10 to get zero and a remainder 3.) On the base, 2, 327 would appear as 101000111 as can easily be shown by dividing successively by 2. In this way a simpler notation is achieved inasmuch as only two signs are used in place of ten. On the other hand the notation is longer since nine figures are used in place of 3. The explicit expression is: $1.2^8 + 0.2^7 + 1.2^6 + 0.2^5 + 0.2^4 + 0.2^3 + 1.2^2 + 1.2^1 + 1.2^0$.

The nature of the base is not essential; the base can easily be changed according to a rule. The same whole number can, therefore, be represented in several ways—in principle in an infinite number of ways. The representations are equivalent inasmuch as they all refer to the same object.

To clarify this point let us consider the case of the rational numbers which are often represented as fractions. A rational number is an ordered pair of integers. Consider the rational number 2/3. This is the ordered pair (2:3); it may be represented by the ordered pair (4:6) or the pair (6:9) etc. . . This rational number itself is whatever is common to all its representations. In general a rational number is the class of ordered pairs of integers (a:b) (a and b being integers) equivalent by the relation $ab' = ba'$. (This relation is the condition of the fractions a/b and a'/b' being equal.) In the present example: $2.6 = 4.3$, $2.9 = 3.6$, etc.

A rational number may be represented either in the form of an ordinary or a decimal fraction. So the rational number (1:3) is represented either as 1/3 or as 0.333. . . This shows the need to distinguish signification and denotation. For there are two significations: on the one hand, a relation between two whole numbers, and, on the other hand, a periodic infinite decimal expansion. But the denotation of the two expressions is the same; they both have the same object. The unity of denotation can be formally stated. If 1 is divided by 3 the result is 0.333··· And if the decimal number 0.333··· is written in explicit fashion one arrives at:

$$3.10^{-1} + 3.10^{-2} + 3.10^{-3} + \cdots$$
$$= 3.10^{-1} (1 + 10^{-1} + 10^{-2} + \cdots\cdot)$$
$$= 3.10^{-1} \left(\frac{1}{1 - 10^{-1}} \right)$$
$$= 3.10^{-1} \cdot \frac{10}{9} = \frac{3}{9} = \frac{1}{3}$$

These examples show that the symbol as instrument of designation appears at the same time as necessary and as inessential. It is necessary inasmuch as it is the only means available for denoting a rational number, which itself is defined in terms of objects whose existence is already assured, and which, accordingly, is an object of the second degree. It is inessential inasmuch as an infinity of representations is possible. The symbol is necessary as symbol, i.e. generically, but inessential in its specificity inasmuch as it is this symbol.

While still on the topic of designation we can consider an approach which illustrates the operational aspect proper to formal symbolism. The ordinary system of notation used for different integers makes determinate names correspond to different integers which are presupposed as objects in their own right. This is the case whatever the base. But, instead of proceeding in this way, the whole numbers may be generated in the act of naming them. Naturally this will be achieved through symbols. For instance, let there be a non-defined object, *o*, a non-defined predicate, *S*, and an operation, the application of the predicate *S* to a term. By *term* will be meant an expression of the type $SS\cdots So$. (The object *o* corresponds to the ordinary *zero* and the predicate *S* to the notion *successor of*. The precise meanings of the symbols *S* and *o* must be fixed by appropriate axioms.) By applying the predicate *S* to the object *o*, by means of the operation of application, and then applying the predicate *S* to the term thus obtained and so on, an unlimited series of objects which one can recognise as integers is reached: *o, So* (the successor of *o* and so 1), *SSo* (the successor of the successor of *o*, so 2) etc. The ordinary symbols (0, 1, 2, 3···) now become simply abbreviations for expressions of the type $SS\cdots So$. Thus we have a regular generative procedure based on the repetition of a given operation which is indefinitely repeatable. In the repeatability of the operation of application (of the predicate *S*) is rediscovered the infinity characteristic of the series of integers.

3.   ALGEBRA

To carry our enquiry a step further we may consider algebra. Take a simple example of algebraic reasoning: the discovery of the fourth proportional. There are three quantities a, b, c (these symbols are simply names for quite determinate numbers). Introduce an unknown quantity, x. The problem may be to determine the value of x when one knows that a is to b as x is to c. By multiplication: x = a c/b. Since the values of a, b, and c are known, the value of x can be determined by the operations of elementary arithmetic.

The role of the symbol in this case is more complex than in designation. For when it is brought into play it designates a magnitude which is not known directly as such but only in its relations to other magnitudes. Algebraic reasoning consists in treating this magnitude in the same way as the others, in behaving as if it were already known. But in order to act thus, a substitute must be found for the magnitude. The symbol occurs to take the place of the thing itself; it is no longer a representation, in the sense of a name, but a substitute. Rigour would require a distinction between the substitute itself and its name. But the important point is that it is impossible to operate on this vicarious object except through the intermediary of symbolic representation. The symbol is always a name, if you will, but the name of a phantom.

The fecundity of this algebraic method is well known. By relying on the fiction of the 'already known', thought successfully resolves problems involving only arithmetical operations (the four fundamental operations, the raising to powers, the extraction of roots). The reason behind the efficacy of the method is that the 'unknown' which is at the centre of the algebraist's speculations figures in operations undertaken according to rules.

All of which suggests a consideration of the operations in themselves. For instance, addition. It has certain properties, e.g. commutivity (a + b = b + a), associativity [a + (b + c) = (a + b) + c], and one can undertake a study of these properties and their formal characteristics. From this viewpoint, addition is an operation by which one can combine two elements to get a third and which has certain formal properties. Bringing to light what is proper to the operations of arithmetic leads to the viewpoint of abstract algebra, which studies sets endowed with operations such as addition, which have the characteristics of 'laws of composition' (they 'compose' an element by means of two given elements) and whose properties are specified. Naturally the operations have to do with objects but these objects are of no importance in themselves. They are designated by means of letters, but are not otherwise determined than by the conditions imposed on them by the characteristic properties of operations. They serve as support—one might almost say decoration—to the operations. The support is clearly non-essential. One and the same algebraic structure can be realised on a multiplicity of supports, and even on supports which, from certain points of view are profoundly dissimilar, e.g. supports constituted by a finite or an infinite number of elements.

4.   LOGIC

It is not a great step from algebra to logic. Take the following proposition: 'The ploys of formal thinking are sewn with white thread'. Isolate the subject: 'The ploys of formal thinking'. The term 'formal thinking' can be replaced by the symbol x to yield: 'The ploys of x'. The x can, of course, stand for formal thinking, but it could equally well stand for Julius Caesar, Queen Christina or whatever. The expression 'The ploys of x' is no longer a noun designating a determinate object. It is a form (which can become a noun as soon as x is replaced by a noun, e.g. by 'Julius Caesar'). Similarly, the whole subject-expression can be replaced by y to give: 'The y are sewn with white thread'. The expression is no longer a proposition but a form which can become a proposition when the symbol y is replaced by a noun. Such a form is neither true nor false. Contrariwise, the proposition obtained by substituting a noun for y is true or false, according as the predicate 'sewn with white thread' is or is not apt. Such a form is a propositional function—an expression which can become a proposition as soon as a value is given to the variable y, that is when y is replaced by a noun.

In this context symbols appear as variables rather than as unknowns. They are terms which can be given different *values*—that is, terms that can be replaced by determinate nouns or predicates. Logical functions are constructed on the model of mathematical functions and symbols play an analogous role. Take the function *sine*. The expression *sin x* is a pure form which can become a determinate real number, between −1 and +1, as soon as the symbol (the *variable*) x is replaced by the designation of a determinate angle. Of course a variable does not have meaning except in reference to a domain constituted by the set of objects which can be substituted for it. In the case of a mathematical function this domain is a mathematical set (for example the set of real numbers). In the case of the propositional functions of logic, the domain is the universe of discourse: the set of individuals on which an utterance may bear. A variable is not, then, in any case, a name.

With the introduction of variables the way is open to a formal analysis of language, and, more generally, of formal thinking.

5. CALCULUS

The formalisation of language to which the use of logical forms leads may seem a useless and pretentious exercise. In practice, however, it has shown great fecundity; formalisation allows the thematisation of operations and so makes the development of purely algorithmic theories possible. This is apparent in the case of algebra whose theories may be regarded as particular realisations of the algorithmic method. The method has, however, a wide scope; algebraic procedures can be generalised and extended to other domains, e.g. to logical operations.

Consider arithmetical addition. Two numbers can be added 'in intuition' by relying on the intuitive sense of the operation of addition and on the direct grasp of the particular numbers in question. On the other hand, with a symbolism one can practise a purely mechanical addition, after the manner of a calculating machine, by following the appropriate rules. One arrives thus at a result without having to reflect on the meaning of the operations by which one does so; the only requirement is to follow the rules laid down.

The same viewpoint can be adopted in algebra. Recall, for instance, the procedures used in seeking the roots of a system of equations. Logic has many analogies with algebra and there is notable parallelism between algebraic operations and the operations of the logic of propositions, which, naturally, entails a correspondence between algebraic theorems and the logical theorems expressing the properties of operations. Thus the algebraic theorem expressing the distributivity of the product in relation to addition [a. (b + c) = (a . b) + (a . c)] finds its correspondent in the theorem expressing the distributivity of the logical product with respect to the logical sum [A and (B or C) is equivalent to (A and B) or (A and C)]. It is, accordingly, possible to construct a logical calculus which is of the same nature as the calculus of algebra. The fecundity of this calculus is shown, for example, in its implementation in decision theory. Thus, in the logic of propositions the application of the rules of the calculus permits one to reduce any complex proposition to a 'normal form'—that is, a canonical form which includes only the elementary propositions (which are used in the composition of the complex proposition under discussion), their negations, and the signs of conjunction and disjunction. The examination of the normal form allows one to 'decide' if the proposition studied is 'true' or 'false'.

In general the invention of an algorithm is a decisive step. The infinitesimal calculus is a particularly striking case. The idea of the infinitesimal method is extremely old but it never became really fruitful until Leibnitz succeeded in giving it the form of a calculus. What was required was a method of subjecting the infinitely small to manipulation according to rule. How were infinitely small magnitudes to be added? The attempt to deal with this problem led to the notion of the integral as the limit of a sum. How express the infinitely small growth which accedes to a function in the neighbour-hood of a given point? This problem led to the notion of a derivation as limit of a quotient. In defining the operations of integration and derivation it appeared that one was the inverse of the other, as subtraction is the inverse of addition, and as the extraction of the root is the inverse of raising to a power. Once these operations had been rigorously defined it was possible to derive a whole calculus, the importance of which is well known, not only for the development of pure mathematics (from the theory of functions to differential geometry) but also for the development of theoretical physics (in particular, field theory).

6. THE VIEWPOINT OF THE PURE OPERATION

Whatever its utility, the calculus appears at first sight as no more than an instrument. In reality it includes its own speculative content. The calculus is based on the operation and the operation can be thematised. By extracting precisely what makes the calculus powerful, formal thinking has opened the way to a pure theory of operations which is its most brilliant achievement to date. Three stages can be distinguished in the process of thematisation which moves from the calculus (that is from the operations in so far as they are in use) to the operations in themselves.

In the first stage the operations are still considered as linked to their objects, e.g. in abstract algebra. Names stand for objects operated on (for instance, elements of a *group*). Certainly the objects are relatively indeterminate: they are introduced only by those properties that are expressly implicated in the axioms which specify how they can be operated on (for instance in the axioms of the group). Still they play the role of concrete individuals and the symbols designating them are names. The operation is symbolic but nonetheless related to objects; it is, then, taken concretely, considered like a transformation which changes one entity into another (for example, in the case of an additive group, a pair of elements x and y, is changed into their sum, x + y).

In the second stage the operation is considered as operation. Objects must be abstracted from but it must be shown how the operations could be linked to objects. The place of possible objects must be indicated and to this end a *form* is required. The mechanism of this formalisation is *abstraction*: the operation must be abstracted from the objects to which it applies. Consider how to represent the composed function (for instance, the function composed of 'the square of the logarithm of'). If the two functions are designated as f and g and the argument by x we can write (in the spirit of concrete representation which is that of ordinary mathematics): f (g x). What is characteristic of this formulation is the way in which the terms are grouped. Such a grouping may be represented as follows by using the symbols (a, b and c) which represent any entities (and are not therefore, restricted to functions or numbers): a (b c). To represent the operation of composition one abstracts from the entities operated on by means of the operator of abstraction λ. This gives λ a b c. a (b c) (which may be read: the application of a to the result of the application of b to c, abstracting from a, b and c). If this expression is to be used—that is, if the operation is to be performed on determinate entities, recourse must be had to a rule of concretisation which in the case of a unique element is written: (λ a. a) x = x. (The expression λ a. a corresponds to the identity operator which when applied to an object reproduces the object. The concretisation rule when referring to this operator reads: the identity operator when applied to the object x gives the object x.) If the operator of composition is applied to f, g and x (where f and g are functions and x a numerical argument) we obtain by concretisation: (λ abc. a (bc)) fgx = f (gx). Thus we return to concrete representation. (For example, if f is the function *square of*, g the function *logarithm*, and x a real number, then the operation of composition when applied to these entities gives the composed function: *square of the logarithm of the real number x*.)

An expression such as λ a b c. a (b c), constructed by means of the operator of abstraction is not simply a name for the operation of composition. It has itself operative scope since it lends itself to a calculus: there are rules permitting its construction (rules of abstraction) and rules permitting its application (rules of concretisation). The use of these rules allows the generation of increasingly complex operations in a purely algorithmic way.

For simplicity's sake, let λ a b c. a (b c) = B. Let f be the function *square of* and g the function *logarithm of*. Bfg is then the composed function *square of the logarithm*. The expression, when applied to the argument x, (Bfgx), gives *the square of the logarithm of x*. Other composed functions can be made, e.g. Bff is *the square of the square*. By simply applying the rules the operation B can be repeated, which permits the composition of a function of one argument with a function of two arguments. Let f be the function *square of* and g the function *product*. Apply B to f to get *the square of a function of one argument*. Apply B to (Bf), g, x and y (where x and y are. for example, integers). This gives:

$$B (Bf) g x y = (Bf) (gx) y$$
$$= Bf (gx) y$$
$$= f [(gx) y]$$
$$= f (gxy),$$

that is, *the square of the product of x and y*.

The expression B (Bf) signifies: *the square of a function of two arguments*. The possibilities of repetition are endless.

A third step involves the elimination of all references to objects, to obtain a pure theory of operations in which it is no longer necessary to employ variables (as in the preceding stage when abstraction was represented only by means of variables). This is the viewpoint of combinatory logic. The entities studied in this logic are *combinators* which represent more or less complex operations defined by their formal properties. Elementary combinators can be introduced intuitively by using abstractive representation. So the combinators W (doubling) and C (inversion) can be introduced as follows:

$$W = \lambda \text{ a b. a b b}$$
$$C = \lambda \text{ a b c. a c b}$$

By the rule of concretisation (when f, g and h represent, e.g., functions) we get:

$$W \text{ f g} = \text{f g g}$$
$$C \text{ f g h} = \text{f h g}$$

However the combinators can be defined without any reference to abstractive representation, in a wholly intrinsic fashion. Certain basic combinators are defined axiomatically and the others are explicitly defined as a function of these. The basic system can be supposed as formed of three combinators: B (composition), W (doubling), C (inversion), defined by the appropriate axioms. Thence can be defined other combinators, e.g. S, allowing the representation of the function *successor of*.

Intuitively S may be defined as: $S = \lambda \text{ a b c. a c (b c)}$. By concretisation (when f and g represent functions and x an argument): $S \text{ f g x} = \text{f x (g x)}$. However S can be defined in terms of B, C and W: $S = B [B (BW) C] (BB)$. (One can convince oneself of this intuitively by having recourse to abstractive representation.)

The objective of combinatory logic is to explore as completely as possible the domain of combinators and to extend as far as possible the representation of formal entities (mathematical or logical) in terms of combinators. The field covered up to now by the methods of combinatory logic is that of effective operations—that is, of operations which in all cases lead to a result in a finite number of steps. This does not cover the entire domain of the operations but it is a basic section of it, the exact knowledge of which is indispensable from many viewpoints. In particular, the operations of this sector intervene in the calculus regarding application, for applied knowledge is dominated by effectiveness. None the less, besides what is effective, there can be introduced, by means of successive formal extensions, operations which are no longer strictly effective. So types of operations or procedures of definition or demonstration that are not strictly constructive can be formulated by means of successive thematisations and taking the domain of effective operations as the point of departure.

Combinatory logic, as well as providing an instrument for the study of effective operations, is of considerable interest inasmuch as it enables one to analyse the foundations of the systems of ordinary logic, such as the logical theory of predicates or the theory of sets (theories which provide a framework of sufficient scope for the formalisation of mathematics). It is none the less possible that the accomplishment of this task would entail infinite repetition. For, in the foundational enterprise certain contradictions appear in the system of combinatory logic. Their elimination requires the introduction of restrictions, which, if they are to be formalised, lead to the development of a more fundamental system whose rules, in turn, in order to escape contradiction, must be subjected to certain restrictions. It is very probable that this process extends to infinity. This involves us in another problematic which would manifest the essentially non-closable character of formal symbolisation.

7. INTERPRETATION

But leaving aside that question for the moment, we have to show how formal thought returns to experience, to the perceived. For, unless it retained the essential link with experience it would be valueless in the search for truth. It has its own consistency but in the final analysis it is a means. Hence the question of interpretation. It is not possible to establish a one-to-one correspondence between the terms of a formal system and the objects and relations constituting an experiential domain. There is no way—at least not generically—of giving empirical sense to all the operations of formal thought. It is rather the formal system as such, as a general field of operations, that can be interpreted, i.e. as a totality.

To illustrate exactly what this means we must make the notion of formal system more precise. With Curry we can say that a formal system is a set of theorems (utterances considered 'valid', 'endowed with validity') generated by precise rules and concerning non-specified objects. The formulation of the rules constituting the skeleton of a formal system must eschew all recourse to intuition, all appeal to the intuitive meaning of propositions, or to the intuitive meaning of the operations on them (even in the case of purely deductive procedures). More explicitly, a formal system is constituted by a collection of conventions determining sets of objects, propositions and theorems. The set of objects is specified as follows: a collection of elementary objects is given explicitly; these are the atoms of the expressions of the system; and with these is given a number of operations which permit the construction of complex objects by means of the elementary objects. The set of propositions is specified thus: a list of primitive predicates is given together with formational rules which allow the construction of expressions called *propositions* by means of the predicates and the objects of the system. The set of theorems is specified thus: a selection of propositions asserted to be *valid* (the axioms of the system) is given, as well as deductive rules which permit, on the basis of these valid propositions, the discovery of new valid propositions. Operations, formative and deductive rules are formulated so as to answer precise conditions of effectiveness: it must be possible to recognise effectively whether or not a given expression is an object of the system, whether or not a given expression is a proposition of the system, and, finally, whether or not a given series of propositions is a deduction of the system. In general it is not required that the notion of 'theorem' be effective; in other words, the deductive rules need not be so formulated that one can effectively recognise, in all cases, whether or not a given expression, formed by means of the symbols of the system, is a theorem of the system. Systems in which the notion of theorem is effective form a special class: decidable systems.

An elementary example will illustrate the definition. Consider a system permitting the representation of certain elementary properties of arithmetic. We may restrict ourselves to one elementary object, o, and to a single operation, S, (*successor of*). The meaning of this operation is fixed by the following rule: if x belongs to the system, then S x will belong to the system. With a single predicate, $=$, the set of propositions will be given by the following rule: if x and y belong to the system, then x $=$ y is a proposition of the system. Finally, we have a single axiom: o $=$ o. Similarly a single deductive rule: if x $=$ y, then S x $=$ S y. It is immediately clear that within this system the following theorems may be derived: o $=$ o, S o $=$ S o, S S o $=$ S S o, etc. This leads to a more general assertion, a meta-theoretic assertion, concerning the deductive properties of one system: if y is an object of the system, then y $=$ y. Such an assertion is an *epitheorem*.

We may consider the presentations, representations and interpretations of a formal system. The *presentation* of a formal system is a particular enunciation of the constitutive framework of the system, of the set of its defining conventions. It is a particular selection of symbols employed to designate the 'primitive ideas' of the system, namely its elementary objects (or atoms), its operations and its predicates. The *representation* of a system is a correspondence established between the *objects* of the system and certain entities (which may be symbols, numbers, ideas, physical objects, etc.) such that two different entities will correspond with two different objects. Finally the interpretation of a system is a correspondence established between the *propositions* of the system and assertions that have significance independently of the system (whether they constitute the propositions of another system or have an intuitive meaning, e.g. as theorems in an intuitive mathematical theory or as empirical assertions

with respect to some experiential domain). The correspondence need not be such that *all* the propositions of the
system have a translation. An interpretation is said to be
valid if every assertion corresponding to a theorem is true.
According to Curry, a formal system may be considered as
an abstraction from its presentations, its representations and
its interpretations.

The notion of interpretation allows us to relate the purely
formal with the domain of intuition and experience. And a
formal system is not completely understood except in so far as
it is considered in this relativity, i.e. in so far as it is open to
interpretations. An important problem in the study of
formal systems is precisely to determine, as it were *a priori*,
the characteristics of admissible interpretations for the
systems under discussion. To say that the system considered
in itself is an abstraction from its interpretations is not to
eliminate all reference to these interpretations. But the
proper content of these interpretations is bracketed and only
the reference as reference is retained (somewhat as in the
mechanism of abstraction examined above the character of
the objects to which the operation applied is bracketed in
favour of a reference only to possible objects). This bracketing allows the isolation of the formal in its very formality,
but even if abstraction is made of the content, still formalisation essentially involves a necessary relation to a field of
possible interpretation. The formal system includes a
reference to its base at the level of experience where its
meanings are constituted.

8. FRUITFULNESS OF FORMALISM

The preceding considerations have a fundamental meaning:
namely, in complete generality, the relation between formalism and experience. In order to see this relation in the
concrete and discover the strength of formalism in action,
we shall consider systems which are not completely formalised (although they could be) and in which the link with

experience is more immediate. We shall take two examples; one from physics, the other from the human sciences.

In the formalism of quantum mechanics there appears the notion, the function of state ψ, whose role is fundamental and the interpretation of which raises enormous problems. What is remarkable is that the use of the function ψ is efficacious, regardless of the meaning assigned to it. The function represents globally the state of a physical system. Given a physical system (atom, system of particles, etc.), a function is associated with a determinate state of that system. The function is designated by the symbol ψ whose behaviour is governed by an equation—the equation of evolution—which links the values of the function to different instants and so allows the study of the development of the system over time. It is not possible to make the function ψ correspond with an intuitive content, nor is there any way of associating it indirectly with an observable datum. None the less, by means of this function, it is possible to obtain useful information on the system studied and to make predictions with respect to it—predictions which are verifiable. Naturally this implies some link between the function ψ and experience. The link may be described as follows:

(*a*) To every physical magnitude, to every observable, there is made to correspond an *operator* which acts on the function ψ, that is a symbol of operation which, when applied to the function ψ, transforms it into another function. (For instance the operator of derivation with respect to time replaces the function ψ by its derivative with respect to time.)

(*b*) The only possible values of a measure effected on an observable will be the *eigenvalues* of the operator associated with this observable. These *eigenvalues* are real numbers, solutions of the eigenvalues equation:

$$A \, \psi = a \, \psi$$

where A is the operator associated with the observable, ψ is the function of state and a is a variable whose values are real numbers.

(The eigenvalues of the operator A are the real number a; corresponding to the functions ψ_i, such as:

$$A \, \psi_i = a_i \, \psi_i$$

The probability of finding in the state ψ, the value a_m for a measure effected on the observable studied is given by the square of ψ_m (ψ_m being the function which corresponds to a_m in the eigenvalues equation).

(*c*) If a series of measurements is carried out on an observable, the mean value is given by an expression in which is found only the function of the state of the system and the operator associated with the observable studied.

Once an operator A has been selected, the state of a system may be described by means of functions of state associated with that operator by the eigenvalues equation (and named eigen functions of this operator). This is the principle of spectral decomposition which gives a probabilist interpretation of the function ψ. The state described by the function ψ appears as the superposition of states described by the functions ψ_i; eigen functions of the operator A; each of these states corresponds to an eigenvalue of the operator A, therefore to a possible measure of the magnitude represented by this operator. More exactly, the function ψ is expressed in the form of a sum of terms each of which is the product of one of the functions ψ_i by a coefficient b_i; and the probability of finding the value a_i corresponding to ψ_i for the observable is given by the square of b_i.

A particular case of the principle of spectral decomposition is the principle of localisation according to which the probability of finding a particle described by the function ψ, in an element of volume dv is given by the product of the square of ψ by dv.

Our second example is the analysis of the Murngin kinship system made by A. Weil on the basis of C. Lévi-Strauss' suggestions. Weil has succeeded in giving a mathematical description of the functioning of this complex kinship system by using relatively simple algebraic tools: the theory of finite groups of transformations and the theory of congruences. He has managed to express algebraically the condition of a society being reducible—i.e. decomposable into at least two groups such that no affinal link may be established between individuals who do not belong to the same group. And he has been able to show that Murngin society is reducible (in so far as it applies its marriage rules strictly). Now this fact was not at all apparent to the observer: the two groups into which Murngin society can be (theoretically) reduced do not at all correspond to the indigenous classifications. What we are faced with is an unavoidable consequence of the application of the rules but a consequence so far removed from the premises that it cannot be as such accessible to observation. It is only when the theoretic analysis on the basis of the mathematical model has been done that it is possible to proceed to verification. When the theoretic predictions are confronted with the ethnological facts, the condition of reducibility is not verified, which demonstrates that the Murngin do not apply their rules strictly. But they are not aware of this. Once again it is only by having recourse to formal representation that the ethnologist makes the discovery.

9. SIGNIFICATION OF FORMAL SYMBOLISM

The fruitfulness of the formal system and its application to experience shows the formal to be revelatory of meaning and to be the locus of a logos. But this meaning is not intuitively grasped nor can it be translated, at least directly, into the discourse of natural language. Formal language is required for the meaning to appear. And formal language is inseparable from symbolic manipulation. Ambiguity should be avoided here for symbolism may be taken in a broad or narrow sense. In its broad sense the term *symbolism* is taken as the equivalent of *formalism*. In the narrow sense the term designates simply the usage made of symbols (understood materially) in the construction of formalisms. More precisely (in Curry's terminology) it refers to the *representation* of a formal system. Now representation is not essential; a formal system must present itself in the guise of a representation, and in general this will be under the guise of a symbolic game (in the narrow sense), but in itself it is distinct from its representations. We may say that symbolism in the broad sense transcends symbolism in the narrow sense, as the essence transcends its manifestations.

At first sight, formalism represents a standstill in thought: it is system frozen, spread out for inspection, strictly determined, a set of procedures established once for all. However, the domain of formalism is not exhausted in its presentation. In fact formalism is essentially linked to the power of operation; it is incessant operation, an infinite matrix of transformation. From this point of view it may be compared to a calculating machine (of course, from other viewpoints, it goes beyond anything represented by such a machine). The meaning of the machine is the totality of its possible operations, but it is always in action, always in the course of an operation; accordingly, its meaning is being continually elaborated. If the formal system is a vehicle of signification, it is not so in the same way as a dictionary in which significations are given once for all. Rather it is a vehicle of signification as a process: as the operations are accomplished the meaning is constructed and there is no *a priori* limit to this genesis.

Some questions emerge. Is formalism merely a technique, a device by which we manage to understand reality better? Is it a locus *sui generis* of the revelation of meaning? Is it the manifestation of a logos of the world which appears through the symbols? Correlative to these questions are others: is the sensible the prime location of truth, or is it merely that which evokes the invention of truth, the exterior pretext for the revelation of the logos?

Further, whatever the relationship between formal thought and sensible experience, is the formal logos the whole of the logos? This question is that of the signification of logic. A superficial view would have it that logic is simply the set of rules governing coherent discourse. But what is discourse, what is speaking? As Heidegger shows, it is a 'bringing together' which makes appear, which makes manifest, which brings things into presence. More exactly, it is an act of selection and liaison which accompanies things in their coming to presence, which, with them, retraces the way of their manifestation. The movement that inhabits discourse is the same movement that inhabits world, it is its setting forth, its original blossoming, its genesis and its growth. 'Logos' is 'physis'. But 'physis' is itself 'ousia', it is that which brings things into presence; it is generative of the universal parousia. As such it indicates how things are called into the partaking of presence, into the confines of being. Logic is thus also ontology.

Yet its meaning remains ambiguous. In the end we are brought back to the question of the relationship between the formal and the sensible. Is logic only the hidden woof, the immanent texture, the secret architecture, of the sensible world, so that it is finally in the splendour of visible things that the shining forth of truth is exhausted? Or is it not rather the imperious movement of truth, its triumphant affirmation, rising from the sensible as light from shadow, abandoning the visible to the dead weight of its own opacity, to the insignificance of its derisory existence? Is it in the life of forms that the destiny of meaning is accomplished? Is the perishable nature of the world but a passing moment in an infinite fall? Or, contrariwise, is it in the obtuseness of the concrete that we find the only access to the fullness of meaning, of which the signs of the world and the mystery of symbols give us but a presentiment and a sketch? Form is not, in any case, frozen; the concrete is not closedness. Perhaps between things and forms, between names and figures, between sign and substance, there is increasing traffic, a universal and permanent symbolisation.

III

The Neo-Positivist Approach

I. INTRODUCTION

During the course of its recent development science has insisted on breaking free from all—or at least all explicit—philosophic or theological presuppositions and has worked out for itself its basic concepts and methodological instruments. So much so that it can now be said that science has been largely successful in establishing itself on its own terms. It remains the case that there are implicit presuppositions in science which can be teased out only by philosophical enquiry but this philosophic elucidation can be achieved only after the science has developed. What is of capital importance is that in its unfolding science makes no appeal to already accepted philosophic conceptions. Metaphysical questions are thus bracketed.

None the less, the practice of science has been the inspiration of a theory of knowledge, neo-positivism, which would not only isolate the domain of science from that of metaphysics, a perfectly acceptable undertaking, but which would go so far as to wholly exclude metaphysics from the field of knowledge. Neo-positivism is not content with affirming that scientific method is incompetent to deal with the classical problems of metaphysics, which could legitimately be held by any epistemology of science in conformity with the intentionality of science, but asserts that these problems are meaningless.

2. THE *Tractatus*

The neo-positivist position in metaphysics is based on a theory of meaning which originates in Wittgenstein's *Tractatus Logico-Philosophicus* (1922). According to the *Tractatus*, language constitutes a picture of the world, an image of reality. Between language and world there is rigorous parallelism. World is the set of states of affairs; its constitutive unities, accordingly, are neither things nor properties, but actual situations. Language is the set of propositions and each proposition corresponds to a possible state of affairs. A proposition can be true or false. It is true when it expresses a state of affairs that is actually realised, false when it expresses a non-realised state of affairs. The set of propositions gives a complete description of the world, since it indicates both the states of affairs that are realised and the states of affairs that are not realised. To know that a proposition is false, that a given state of affairs is not realised, is to know something about the world. The truth value of a proposition must be distinguished from its meaning; before being classified as true or false a proposition must have a meaning. The meaning of a proposition is its possibility of being recognised as true or false. In other words, the meaning of a proposition is the circumstances which allow the discovery of its truth or falsity—or, more simply, its verification conditions.

According to this criterion of meaning only scientific propositions are meaningful. These propositions describe reality, the world as it is. Still, besides descriptive propositions there are other propositions which have a role in scientific language and yet do not express states of affairs— namely, purely logical propositions. These propositions have a very special status and are forms rather than strictly propositions. They are expressions containing variables and become propositions only when these variables are replaced with propositions strictly so called; they are either tautologous or contradictory. When the variables are replaced by propositions, these expressions are at once either true or false, no matter how the substitution is made—that is, whatever the truth value of the propositions substituted for the variables. These expressions represent admissible forms of reasoning, not states of affairs. They are without meaning since they cannot be associated with a process of verification like propositions (strictly so called). They are not, however, nonsensical: they have a legitimate function in language inasmuch as they are to be applied to meaningful expressions.

There are expressions, however, that are nonsense, mere collections of words with neither meaning nor logical function—namely, the expressions that occur in philosophical discourse. These expressions appear to be propositions but, having no more than the linguistic structure of propositions, they are in fact pseudo-propositions. They do not refer to a possible state of affairs but purport rather to express the generic conditions governing states of affairs and to reach essences or reality. Now discourse about essences or about reality as a whole is not possible. It is true that there is a common element in the proposition and the state of affairs of which it is the image, namely, form. Form is shown in the proposition but it cannot be said; there can be, accordingly, no discourse concerning essences. Similarly, the totality of language describes the totality of world, but there is no language of language, no discourse about discourse; there is, then, no discourse about the totality as such. Wittgenstein notes, however, the 'mystical element' manifested in language—that is, the fact that there is a world, or again that there are conditions which make world possible. Language describes world, expresses the 'how' of world; and through language, that which constitutes the world as world, that which posits world, is shown. What this is cannot be said; there is a presence in language of the reality which is beyond world. There is, then, a going beyond world by means of language but there can be no metaphysical discourse in which this going beyond and this reality could be expressed. What, then, of the statements of the *Tractatus* itself? On their own ground and according to the theory of meaning they put forward they must be considered to be nonsense, as Wittgenstein concludes. Still, they are to be given a paradoxical function for, through this meaninglessness, they lead to a grasp of what cannot be said. Whoever has worked through them and has finally risen above them understands what is the case concerning language and world; he is in the presence of what cannot be spoken of.

By allowing the paradoxical usage of the *Tractatus*, Wittgenstein ends in a sort of logical mysticism, he rejects all explicit metaphysics, all discourse concerning the absolute yet at the same time finds in discourse the means of rising above discourse and reaching the absolute. His position is, therefore, not atheistic; although it rejects the possibility of discourse concerning God's existence, still it opens a way to the recognition of this existence. This way cannot be made explicit in a reasoned and logically coercive argument, but it cannot be termed irrational since it is based on language and on the logical elements in language. It is *exercite* not *signata*, in the realm of performance not content. The orientation is performatively operative within language and consequently within science, since without language there is no science, but it cannot be thematised.

Wittgenstein's position in the *Tractatus* may be accounted for in terms of his theory of propositions. According to this theory there is no unit of sense anterior to the proposition; the constituent terms of the proposition have meaning only in the context of the proposition as a whole. Accordingly, priority is given to the proposition over the concept, which has no proper role as the mind has no direct grasp of the intelligible elements present in reality. So in the proposition there is no question of concepts being applied to reality, for the proposition is simply the image, the linguistic double of reality. As for reality, it is constructed not of relatively isolable individuals endowed with certain properties but of simple totalities, matters of fact. Facts can only be stated, they do not lend themselves to interpretation, to intelligible reconstitution. Propositions are purely descriptive and express a possible *constatation*; they are true when the described facts can be affirmed in fact, false when they cannot. The meaning of a proposition is simply its relation to a possible affirmation, and to the procedure establishing its truth-value. Meaning does not correspond to an intelligible component present in the abstract terms involved in judgment; hence it cannot be thematised and there is no language concerning significations, essences, or the conditions of possibility of facts and world. Language allows the expression of a description of world but not of a thought of world.

3.   VERIFICATION THEORY

Neo-positivism takes over Wittgenstein's theory of meaning but, applying its criteria of verification strictly, rejects everything in the *Tractatus* which suggests a realm beyond language. The neo-positivist position is organised around two basic principles: empiricism and verifiability. Empiricism asserts that the sole legitimate basis of knowledge is sense experience, that only the empirically given can give content to knowledge. Verifiability asserts that the meaning of a proposition lies in the procedures which enable its truth or falsity to be determined. In other words, a proposition has meaning only if it can be verified—at least in principle. (For a proposition to be declared meaningful it is not required that it should have been already verified, nor even that one has the means of verifying it. It is enough if its verification is seen as possible, given the state of science at the time the proposition is stated.) Both principles do not have exactly the same function and are not to be considered as juxtaposed on the same level. Empiricism is basic. Its scope is very general and its formulation is imprecise enough to allow diverse interpretations. Verifiability is a relatively precise criterion which allows one to judge linguistic expression from an empiricist viewpoint. It is the putting into practice on the level of linguistic analysis of the principle of empiricism. While empiricism remains a very generic epistemological demand, serving only to indicate a preferred approach, verifiability pretends to reveal the implications of the generic demand in a more formal and explicit way. Conversely, while the principle of verifiability is only a specification of more basic empiricism, the way in which it is understood will determine the way in which the empiricist postulate is understood.

There have been various interpretations of the verification principle within neo-positivism. It is possible to discern two stages in its growth: in the first stage, which runs from the formation of the Vienna circle (this can be put at 1922 when Moritz Schlick was appointed Professor of the Philosophy of Inductive Science at the University of Vienna) until about 1935, the principle is taken in the strict sense; 1935 or thereabouts saw the emergence of criticisms which influenced the majority of authors to abandon the strict interpretation and to formulate anew the criterion of meaning. Among these new attempts Carnap's was one of the most exact. In *Testability and Meaning* (published in 1936 and 1937 in vols III and IV of *Philosophy of Science*) he suggests in place of verification the idea of confirmation and elaborates the criteria of sense from this basis. As Carnap has been one of the most celebrated members of the neo-positivist movement from its inception and because he has offered particularly rigorous formulations of the neo-positivist position, we can limit ourselves to an examination of his position before and after *Testability and Meaning*.

Consider first the presentation of the verifiability principle in its strict form and its implications in Carnap. The analysis of the processes of thought and of the procedures used in the elaboration of knowledge can be reduced to the analysis of language. In language the unit of meaning is the proposition. The proposition itself is a complex entity containing simpler elements, e.g. the signs of logical operations on the one hand, and, on the other hand, terms which correspond

to concepts. The meaning of the logical operations is determined by the syntactical rules which serve to define them.
As for the meaning of concepts, this is given in what Carnap
calls 'elementary statements'. The elementary statement of a
concept K is the simplest possible propositional form in
which K appears—i.e., an expression of the type 'X is a K',
where X can be replaced by the designation of the object
belonging to a well-determined category of objects (e.g. the
category of physical objects, of persons, of numbers). The
concept K has a meaning if the propositions which can be
elicited from its elementary statement by replacing X by
the designation of a determinate object from an appropriate
category, themselves have meaning. And these propositions
are meaningful if one knows how they may be verified—
that is, if one knows the conditions under which they would
be true, and those under which they would be false. A large
number of concepts may be defined by means of more
elementary concepts and the verification of the elementary
utterances of the former is reduced to the verification of the
latter. Thus one comes closer and closer to concepts whose
elementary statements are in the form of observation statements, whose verification consists in directly observing
certain states of affairs. Their verification comes down to
purely empirical constatations.

At the close of this analysis one is led to reject all metaphysical concepts as meaningless. Take the concept 'God'.
This concept can be understood, mythologically, metaphysically, or theologically. Understood mythologically it
has a meaning: it refers either to corporeal beings endowed
with special properties, or to spiritual beings who reveal
themselves in some fashion in the visible world and have,
accordingly, an empirically verifiable mode of existence.
Understood metaphysically the concept is meaningless. No
matter how the concept is introduced, the truth conditions
of its elementary statement are never given and no attempt
is made to indicate precisely to what category the objects
to be substituted for the variable X in the elementary

statement should belong. As for theological understanding, it occupies the middle ground between the two preceding positions. If the theological notion of God is taken empirically, then the statements in which it appears are susceptible to experimental scientific control; if the notion is taken metaphysically, then the statements in which it appears are meaningless and so the notion itself is meaningless. Similar criticisms can be made of other metaphysical concepts such as 'being', 'absolute', 'first cause', in itself', etc.

Let us turn to the presentation of the conditions of meaning for propositions in general. Distinguish analytic and synthetic propositions. Analytic propositions are true or false as a function of their form alone, independent of any relation to a content or external datum. True analytic propositions are tautologies; false analytic propositions are logical contradictions. The propositions of logic and mathematics are tautologous: they have no real content and tell us nothing about reality. They simply indicate possible intellectual operations on propositions of real cognitive import, on the contents of knowledge. Synthetic propositions are those in which the attribution of predicate to subject is the result of a synthesis, of a real link which is not based simply in the meaning of the terms used. Such propositions can be based only on experience. They have meaning only in so far as they lend themselves to direct or indirect empirical verification, so that either they are directly testable observation statements, or one can judge their truth or falsity by referring to directly verifiable observation statements. Consequently only scientific statements are meaningful. Metaphysical propositions which purport to speak of meta-empirical beings or conditions are nothing more than pseudo-propositions—that is, collocations of words without significance.

Metaphysical statements are apparently meaningful in that they are constructed according to the rules of syntax and are, then, to be distinguished from verbal collocations such as 'the table is since' which do not form propositions

6

and consequently can have no meaning. But the rules of grammar are far from being complete and fail to exclude such manifestly senseless utterances as 'Caesar is a prime number' and, *a fortiori*, metaphysical statements which are apparently meaningful, but in reality, in terms of the foregoing analysis, vacuous. A complete syntax would have to eliminate pseudo-propositions and in order to do this it would have to specify to what syntactic category the terms united in a proposition would have to belong. So in the example 'Caesar is a prime number' we are not dealing with a real proposition because the predicate 'prime number' can be applied only to objects belonging to the syntactic category number. A rigorous and complete syntax, constructed in conformity with the criterion of verifiability, would automatically exclude all pseudo-propositions, including all metaphysical utterances.

Does this mean that all philosophy is to disappear? No. In one area philosophy is possible and legitimate, namely an objective study of the conditions and procedures of science, and since science is expressed in language this study will take the form of a meta-language thanks to which it will be possible to subject the properties of scientific language to a theoretic examination. Philosophy thus becomes philosophy of science and the philosophical analysis of science is the meta-language of science, the meta-linguistic study of scientific language. Carnap at first identified the meta-language of science with the syntax of scientific language —that is, with the study of the intrinsic properties of that language, its rules of formation and deduction and all that they imply. Later, together with syntax he introduced semantics which was to be the study of the relations between linguistic expressions and the states of affairs they described. To semantics fell the task of elucidating such notions as truth and verification. Syntax and semantics have a purely logical side which studies the formal properties of language and is characteristically *a priori*, and a descriptive side which studies the actual properties of language (more precisely of the concrete languages which are the object of study) and is characteristically empirical.

Meta-linguistic methods enable one to analyse the mechanisms which gave rise to the pseudo-propositions of metaphysics and to reveal the confusions at their base. Consider, for instance, the Cartesian 'Cogito, ergo sum'. In the proposition 'ergo sum' existence is obviously considered as a predicate. Now, logically, a proposition concerning existence should be analysed thus: 'There is an object with such and such properties'. In other words, existence can be attached only to a predicate, and not to a term designating an individual. The consideration of existence as a predicate flows from a false interpretation of existential propositions. If this is the case, then not merely is the proposition 'I exist' misinterpreted, but the argument of the 'Cogito' founders. From the proposition 'I think' cannot be deduced the proposition 'I am' but only the proposition 'There is something that thinks'.

More generally, syntactic analysis shows that the pseudo-propositions of metaphysics have their source in a confusion, suggested by certain forms of language, between object propositions and syntactic ones. Object propositions express properties and relations belonging to objects in the domain under investigation; they are part of the language relating directly to objects. Syntactic propositions express the properties of this language. Furthermore, there is a third class of propositions between the two preceding types— namely, the class of object pseudo-propositions. These have the same form as object propositions, but they really express syntactic properties, they are quasi-syntactic propositions. The construction of such propositions is made possible by what Carnap calls the material mode of language (in contra- distinction to the formal mode to which properly syntactic propositions belong). A proposition is in the material mode when it attributes to an object a a property P which is the equivalent of a syntactic property—that is, more precisely, when there exists a syntactic property which belongs to the (syntactic) designation of the object *a* if and only if the property *P* belongs to the object *a*. As an example, consider 'Five is a prime number'. This is an object proposition within arithmetical language. We can erect the syntactic proposition: ' "Five" is not the name of a thing, it is the name of a number'. In this proposition, the expression 'Five', formed by the word *five* within inverted commas, is used as a designation for the object constituted by the number *five*. It is a (syntactic) name for this object. We can also erect the quasi-syntactic proposition: 'Five is not a thing, but a number'. This proposition has the form of an object proposition, but in fact it is no more than the expression in the material mode of what is expressed in the formal mode by the syntactic proposition which we have just examined. It attributes to the object *five* the property 'being a number' which is equivalent (in the sense explained above) to the syntactic property 'being the name of a number'. The material mode is not in itself unacceptable but it can easily lead to misunderstandings, from which philosophical problems emerge. The true context of a quasi-syntactical proposition in the material mode is revealed in its syntactic translation. But if the quasi-syntactic proposition is taken as an object proposition (which is what it seems to be) then one is led to formulate pseudo-questions which vanish once the true character of the proposition is understood. So the real content of the proposition: 'A thing is a complex of sensible data' is the content of the syntactical proposition: 'Every proposition in which appears the designation of a thing is equivalent to a class of propositions in which appears no designation of things but only designation of sensible data'. (The example is taken from Carnap: *The Logical Syntax of Language*, 1934, in which the author works out the theory of quasi-syntactic propositions.) If the proposition is taken at its face value there arise the pseudo-questions on the nature of things. Meta-linguistics, by clarifying language, eliminates pseudo-questions of this kind and does away with the misunderstandings that give rise to metaphysical discourse.

4. CONFIRMABILITY, TESTABILITY, TRANSLATABILITY

In *Testability and Meaning* Carnap deals with the various criticisms brought against his theory of verifiability and suggests a new theory of meaning which takes them into account. If one examines closely the conditions which allow one to determine the truth or falsity of a proposition, it becomes clear that it is not possible to speak rigorously of either verification or verifiability. This is evident in the case of universal propositions like a scientific law, the verification of which would demand an examination of all the concrete instances covered by the law which would imply an indefinitely protracted enquiry. Careful attention reveals the same situation in the case of a particular proposition like 'There is a piece of white paper on the table'. To assure the truth of this kind of proposition other propositions which would suggest observations which in turn would serve as predictions with respect to future observations, must be deduced from it. At least in principle the number of these predictions is infinite; even if in practice one is normally content to verify only a few, it would be theoretically possible to continue the process of verification indefinitely and thus indefinitely augment the degree to which the proposition might be considered as true. The verification is not an 'all or nothing' affair, which once undertaken leads to a definite result in a finite time. It is, on the contrary, an operation which is in principle of indefinite length and which, at each stage, yields an answer corresponding to some degree of certainty. Instead of speaking of verification, therefore, one should speak of confirmability. To give this idea a precise content Carnap proposes different criteria of meaning in conformity with the principle of empiricism which may be considered as acceptable formulations of this principle.

The criteria involve the notion of *descriptive predicate*. As the term itself suggests, this is a predicate expressing an observable aspect of a given state of affairs. The most important class of predicates of this type and the only ones considered by Carnap (although his analysis could be easily extended to cover other classes of descriptive predicates) is the class of predicates attributable to points in the space-time continuum, or to small regions of space-time. Carnap's criteria also involve *observable predicates* and *realisable predicates*. A predicate *P* is said to be *observable* for a determinate observer if, for a suitable argument *a*, this observer is capable in appropriate circumstances of obtaining from the proposition '*a* possesses the property *P*' or its opposite '*a* does not possess the property *P*' such confirmation as will lead him either to accept or reject the proposition '*a* possesses the property *P*'. A predicate *P* is said to be *realisable* for a determinate observer if, for a suitable argument *a*, the observer is capable in appropriate circumstances of making the proposition '*a* possesses the property *P*' true—that is, of effecting the appearance of the property *P* at the point designated by the term *a*. Carnap's criteria are formulated for a language which is considered to contain only descriptive predicates.

Corresponding with the distinction between *observable* and *realisable* predicates, there is a distinction between *confirmable* and *testable* propositions. A proposition will be said to be *completely confirmable* if each (descriptive) predicate in the proposition is wholly reducible to a class of observable predicates—that is, if one can reduce a decision concerning the link between this predicate and an individual *a*, to decisions concerning the link between this individual and a class of observable predicates. A proposition will be called *confirmable* if the process of confirmation cannot be completed in a finite number of stages. A proposition will be called *completely testable* if it is completely confirmable and if, in addition, all the (descriptive) predicates appearing in the proposition are completely testable—that is, if methods of testing can be designated which would allow one to decide for each predicate whether or not it belonged to this or that individual, and would allow one to decide this in a finite number of stages. If the process cannot be completed in a

finite number of stages then the proposition will be referred
to as *testable*. The difference between confirmability and
testability is that the former demands only the possibility
of confirmation, while the latter requires that one can arrive
at a judgement concerning the truth-value of the tested
proposition. The essential point, and here the principle of
empiricism makes its appearance—is that the confirmation
process must rely on empirical statements which are
either realisable in principle or effectively and concretely
practicable.

Carnap's four criteria can be set out in order of decreasing
strictness. The most demanding criterion is complete testability: 'Every synthetic proposition must be completely
testable'. This implies that one possesses a testing method
which allows the determination for appropriate points and
for each (descriptive) predicate in the proposition whether
or not the predicate belongs to these points. There is the
further implication that one limit oneself to those propositions which do not contain quantifiers (i.e. logical operators
such as 'for every object' or 'for some object'). By substituting
for the notion of testability the less demanding confirmability, the criterion of complete confirmability is obtained:
'Every synthetic proposition must be completely confirmable'. This implies that for every (descriptive) predicate in
the proposition and for appropriate points it will be possible
to determine whether or not the predicate belongs to these
points. It implies too that one is limited to propositions
without quantifiers. If the condition with respect to quantifiers is dropped, two further criteria are obtained. First,
testability: 'Every synthetic proposition must be testable'.
Second, confirmability: 'Every synthetic proposition must be
confirmable'. This last is the most liberal of the four; it is
none the less perfectly conformable with the general prescription outlined in the principle of empiricism and can be
taken as an empiricist criterion in this sense.

As Hempel (in *Problems and Changes in the Empirical Criterion
of Meaning*, 1950) noted, Carnap's position in *Testability and*

Meaning leads to a criterion of meaning based on translatability: a proposition will be considered meaningful if and only if it is translatable into empirical language. For this criterion to be precise it is necessary to determine the conditions which an empirical language must meet, and these conditions may be selected with greater or less strictness but always in line with this general directive: all the propositions of an empirical language must be expressible, by means of the ordinary logical operations, in terms of observable characteristics which can belong to physical objects. If one accepts a theory of meaning of this kind, one is led to discover that the meaning content of a proposition is not uniquely determined by the observation statements to which the proposition can be reduced, but also by the set of logical relations between all the propositions within the language to which the proposition under consideration belongs. In other words, the relation between a meaningful proposition and its empirical base is less simple than was originally thought by the positivists. A proposition must be attached to the totality of the language of which it is a part and it is the language itself, in its totality, which must be constructed according to empiricist criteria. This new interpretation of the empiricist theory of meaning has precisely the same import as the earlier theory as far as metaphysics is concerned. According to the criterion of translatability, metaphysical propositions are meaningless just as they are according to the criteria of verifiability, confirmability or testability.

5.   EMPIRICISM AND CONCEPTUALISM

What is basically and in the first place open to question in neo-positivism is the principle of empiricism itself. Only later may the derivative theory of meaning be examined. The principle can be understood in a very general sense as the assertion that all knowing is linked to sense experience, which comes down to the elimination of intellectual intuition as a possible source of knowledge. But the role of sense experience has still to be determined, and one can adopt either the strict empiricist position of the neo-positivists or a conceptualist position. From the strict empiricist position our knowledge refers exclusively to facts and its content is reduced to whatever is given in sense data. Logical operations allow the organising of these data and the construction on this basis of a science, a systematic body of knowledge, but the content of the science is limited by the data which it organises. From the conceptualist position, intelligence is considered capable of grasping intelligible contents in the sensible data. These contents go beyond the datum as such and enable one to understand it. The field of experience is not limited by sense experience for there is also experience of the intelligible. However, the intelligible is not the object of direct vision—conceptualism is empiricist in so far as it rejects intellectual intuition—and cannot grasp the intelligible aspects of reality, which are expressed in concepts, except in association with sense experience. The intelligible is immanent in the sensible. The concept, which is the intellectual instrument by which and in which we attain the intelligible, does not present us with a reality other than that given in perceptual experience but it makes us grasp the reality differently. In it we attain to meaningful contents, to kernels of signification that perception includes but does not thematise.

Now, if a conceptualist epistemology is accepted, then an interpretation of propositions very different from the neo-positivist interpretation is demanded. The proposition will no longer be regarded as a linguistic expression referring directly or indirectly to a state of affairs but as the expression of a judgement. Judgement is the intellectual act by which we confer on reality (represented by the subject) the intelligible predicates that we have grasped in reality and that we have considered apart from it, as it were isolated considered in themselves and for themselves. Judgement restores the unity of knowledge broken in the act of con-

ception. This unity is based in the unity of the thing itself.
Judgement claims to effect a synthesis conformable to what
reality is in itself, i.e. to present itself as true. Verification
is indeed required to ensure that the judgement succeeds in
attaining its goal but the meaning of the proposition does
not lie in this; the meaning lies rather in the synthesis itself
represented by the proposition, and the meaning of the
synthesis depends on the meaning of its constituent parts
which themselves have meaning inasmuch as they are
carriers of intelligibility.

If it now seems that we can not only invent concepts
relating to particular aspects of reality but also work out
concepts in which we intend the totality as such and the
conditions of its appearing, then we can erect not only a
science but also a metaphysics. For metaphysics is the effort
to work out what is implicit in the grasp of the whole of
reality, considered formally as totality. If we have concepts
in which we attain not this or that determinate content but
the conditions of the existence of things and of the fact that
we possess determinate contents, then it will be possible by
following the way indicated by these concepts to constitute
a metaphysical discourse. In particular it will be possible
by showing what is implied in these concepts, by demonstrating that they include an affirmation of the absolute and
by reflecting on the relations between this absolute and the
finite reality of our experience, to ascend progressively by
way of reason to an acknowledgement of God's existence.
If metaphysics is excluded in a strictly empiricist epistemology, it is on the contrary quite possible in a conceptualist
theory of knowledge.

It remains to be seen whether or not neo-positivist
epistemology does in fact conform to the experience of
scientific thinking. On a first showing it would seem that
the empiricist postulate in its strict form expressed adequately
the intellectual intentionality of science. But would the
conceptualist theory not fit the facts of scientific practice
better? In their criticism of the first formulation of the

verification principle the neo-positivists themselves noted that empirical observations yielded no more than confirmation—more often partial confirmation—of propositions that can be formulated, and that propositions are to be regarded more as anticipations than as descriptions of experience. In brief, there is a priority of thought over fact. In their interpretation of this situation they attributed this anticipatory power to language. But language is the expression of the strategies of thought. Are these strategies purely formal? How is one to explain an ability to anticipate experience, and the at least partial ratification of an anticipation if our thought is not, as such, oriented to the facts? Conceptualism would explain this fecundity of thought by saying that the human mind is capable of grasping in the reality presented to perception intelligible elements that can be thematised and considered for themselves. Once a concept has been worked out we can by means of it intend a not-yet-present reality; we can thus anticipate experience. Of course the verdict of experience is required to justify this intention, to allow us eventually to correct or complete it, to allow us to make critical use of our concepts. But it is not this recourse to experience that gives meaning to our concepts. Contrariwise, the concept gives meaning to experience, makes it accessible to mind, opens it to understanding. Equipped with the concept, we tackle experience and illuminate it. If there is meaning, it is because there is the intelligible. And the intelligible is not exhausted by science. Besides the particular, there is the totality; besides scientific discourse there is metaphysical discourse. Far from being an argument against the legitimacy of such discourse, scientific practice seems rather to favour a conceptualist theory of knowledge. If it does not directly furnish an argument in favour of metaphysics at least it makes plausible the existence of a conceptual level in which its own conceptual level would be both thematised and based.

IV

Self-involving Language, Theology and Philosophy

1. EVANS' THEORY OF LANGUAGE AND FAITH

In his *The Logic of Self-Involvement*, a work of remarkable analytic skill, Donald Evans re-examines, in a quite original way, several philosophical, theological and exegetical questions, takes up and supplements Austin's theory of performative language under the rubric of a theory of self-involving language and applies this theory to the analysis of biblical language, and more particularly to a study of the concept of creation in both Old and New Testaments.[1]

It is generally agreed that two stages can be discerned in Austin's theory. In the first stage, Austin contrasts performative utterances with pure statements of fact and characterises the former as utterances which bring about an action. (Thus in saying 'I promise to come tomorrow' I effectively bind myself to coming.) In the second stage, Austin notes the impossibility of finding precise criteria for distinguishing between performative and constative verbs and concludes by considering performativity and constativity as varieties of a single significative force which he names the *illocutionary force*. This is a dimension of signification distinct from sense and reference: it is what I do when I utter a sentence. Every linguistic expression, in the terms of Austin's final theory, includes three aspects: a locutionary

[1]See Donald Evans, *The Logic of Self-Involvement. A Philosophical Study of Everyday Language with Special Reference to the Christian Use of Language about God as Creator*, London: S.C.M. 1963; quoted in this chapter with page references.

aspect (the expression has sense and reference), an illocutionary aspect (the expression has a characteristic force, e.g.
a statement, an order) and a perlocutionary aspect (the
expression brings with it some effects).

Evans takes up Austin's theory in its final form while
modifying the terminology slightly. Instead of the term
'utterance considered in its illocutionary force' he uses the
term 'performative utterance'; he replaces the term 'perlocutionary force' by the term 'causal force' and retains the
term 'constatives' from Austin's first theory to designate
propositions which can be true or false. (In his second theory,
Austin himself replaces 'constatives' by the wider category
'expositives'.) Excepting these differences he accepts Austin's
classifications. Five categories of performatives can be
distinguished:

> constatives, e.g. This book is very valuable;
> commissives, e.g. I promise you my support;
> exercitives, e.g. I dub you knight;
> behabitives, e.g. I thank you;
> verdictives, e.g. I consider your theory very intelligent.

The utterances expressing conduct (behabitives) or commitment (commissives) have a particular characteristic
which makes them self-involving: they carry in their very
meaning a reference to the speaker's behaviour. A behabitive
implicitly presupposes a certain attitude in the speaker; a
commissive implies the speaker's commitment to a general
action. Evans offers a very detailed analysis of these types
of utterances and works out a logic of the relations between
performatives.

Besides the performative use of language, there is causal
and expressive use. A proposition has a causal use in so far
as it brings with it certain effects in the listener—whether
intentionally or not.

On the other hand, a proposition can express a feeling,
an opinion or an intention. Evans works out a wholly
original theory of the expressive use of language which
supplements Austin's theory of performatives. The expres-

sion of an opinion or an intention belongs to performative use, but the expression of feeling constitutes a specific use of language. For behaviour which manifests feeling he uses the term FRB—feeling-revealing behaviour, of which he discerns four kinds: symptoms, manifestations, expressions and reports, and gives a detailed analysis of their differences. The distinctive characteristic of expressions should be noted, namely that, as a general rule, the expression of a feeling forms part of the meaning of the term which designates this feeling and is not replaceable without residue by another expression.

Like behabitives and commissives, expressive language is self-involving. Within his theory of expressive language, Evans introduces the category of rapportive language, which might also be called a language of affinity. An utterance is called rapportive when it cannot be understood unless one has an affinity, a rapport, with the speaker: this is particularly the case when the actions to which the utterances refer are '*expressive* or when their *rationale* is *profound*' (p. 111).[2] Rapportive language is not necessarily self-involving (but can be so).

In many cases, performative language, like expressive language, implies attitudes. Among those expressions which presuppose attitudes Evans reserves a special place for expressions of the type 'I look on a as b'. Such expressions (and their corresponding attitudes) are named 'onlooks'.[3] Evans distinguishes analogical onlooks (I look on music as a language) and parabolic onlooks (I look on Smith as a tool). The similarity discerned between the two terms of a parabolic onlook is based on the similarity in the attitudes appropriate to each term. In analogical onlooks, the similarity is independent of attitude.

We have, then, with respect to language use, a classifica-

---

[2]Ladrière translates Evans' 'rationale' as 'motivation'. I have restored the original rather than give 'motivation'—*translator's note.*

[3]Ladrière suggests 'assimilateurs' as the French for 'onlooks' and uses this in the text. I have retained 'onlooks'—*translator's note.*

tion into three categories: the performative mode, the causal mode and the expressive mode. With respect to the conditions of understanding, we have the distinction between rapportive and non-rapportive language. Self-involving language covers a part of the performative use of language (namely behavitives and commissives) and the totality of the expressive use. Every proposition has a performative aspect and possesses an illocutionary force. An expressive utterance can be—but need not be—a performative; it is 'often rapportive, but it need not be' (p. 114). 'A rapportive utterance may be self-involving; but it may not' (p. 114).

Evans applies this theory of language to the biblical expressions of creation. His basic thesis is that these expressions—indeed the propositions of biblical language in general—are self-involving. He analyses in turn the performative, expressive, and causal aspect of the concept of creation.

Let us consider first the performative aspect. In the Old Testament the creation of the world is presented as similar to the creation of Israel. In the creation of the world, as in the creation of Israel, the creative word of God has simultaneously 'Exercitive, Verdictive and Commissive force' (p. 158). The creature, for his part, recognises his status as a creature by means of behavitives and commissives—that is, in self-involving language. The New Testament adds an important element to the biblical notion of creation: Jesus is the 'divine "word", by whose power and authority the world was created and constituted' (p. 165). Christ's words have a performative character; and the causal efficacy of his utterances 'depends on the response of men' (p. 167), who express their response by correlative performatives.

When, in the second place, we shift our attention to the expressive aspect of creation we have to introduce such terms as 'glory' and 'holiness'. In the Old Testament, Israel and the world (whose creation is similar to that of Israel) manifest the glory and the holiness of God. These terms involve a threefold reference: they express an 'inner divine quality'—which is manifested through 'certain impressive observables'—and these evoke a 'human feeling-response and acknowledgement' (p. 174). The observables are impressive in that they initiate an internal state in whoever perceives them, and expressive in that they manifest an internal divine quality in the same way that a specifically expressive utterance manifests a feeling. In this context Evans introduces the term SRB—soul-revealing behaviour— by which he refers to behaviour which reveals the intimate self of a being. There is an analogy between FRB and SRB, and the analysis of FRB allows us to clarify the status of SRB. In particular when SRB is expressive it 'is part of the meaning of the word which is used to describe' (p. 186) the quality of soul which it reveals, just as expressive FRB is part of the meaning of the term used to report the feelings which it expresses. The meaning of the terms 'glory' and 'holiness' is 'not abstractable from the observables' (p. 187) in which these qualities are expressed. None the less, in themselves, these qualities remain unobservable. 'According to the New Testament, the glory of the world-creator is revealed in Jesus Christ . . . Jesus is related to the glory of God in a threefold way: (i) the inner glory of Jesus is equated with the *inner glory* of God' (p. 204); (ii) Jesus is in some unique and privileged way 'the *observable expression* of God's inner glory; (iii) Jesus is also the man who renders the perfect *acknowledgement* of God's glory, the "perfect obedience which alone is perfect worship"' (p. 205). Evans analyses the role of Christ as the most perfect manifestation of the glory and holiness of God, using his concept of SRB and showing, on the basis of the properties of this concept, how the revelation of divine reality in Jesus Christ is indispensable to a true understanding of God.

The mystery of God, revealed in Jesus Christ, is accessible only to those who are already inspired by the spirit of Christ, already transformed by the divine action. As well as the divine reality of Christ they are able to grasp the founda- tional intention of creation which is 'the revelation fo glory and the bestowal of glory through Jesus' (p. 217). It follows that the biblical language concerning creation is not merely self-involving but rapportive. To understand an utterance such as 'God is creator of the world' presupposes a rapport, an affinity with the Creator-God, because the creative act is expressive, because it is the product of a profound rationale that is available only to one who shares some part of God's inward life.

Thirdly, the causal aspect of the concept of creation must be considered. The causal aspect of the biblical concept of creation should be analysed, according to Evans, in terms of parabolic onlooks. A parable is a message indicating the proper attitude one should have towards God. It suggests that we should consider God as this or that determinate term; the comparison thus established is based on the similarity in the attitudes appropriate to both God and the other term. The parabolic language of the Bible presents God as a metaphysical entity analogous to the human soul. Metaphysical entities, in Evans' view, are 'beings that can only be described in terms of human attitudes which are believed to be appropriate' (p. 226). In an analysis of the image of the potter and of victory (creation as victory over darkness and chaos), Evans shows in some detail how the causal use of biblical language is parabolic. In the parable of the potter, for instance, the utterance 'God formed man' is not a pure constative. Rather it is a parabolic onlook which is furthermore both self-involving and rapportive. We may note that this is necessarily the case with respect to biblical language about creation. When a human action is an exercitive, a verdictive or a commissive, when it is impressive-expressive and when it is profound in rationale, it is described in a language at once performative, expressive and rapportive. But it includes a causal core which can be isolated and expressed in the form of a pure constative. Such is not the case with divine action. The causal element in creation can be spoken of only 'in parables, in language which is both self-involving and rapportive' (p. 250). This

7

does not detract from the 'reality' of the divine action, but 'what is *meant* by "God the Creator" cannot be abstracted from human attitudes' (p. 251).

Evans develops his reflexions on the causal aspect of the concept of creation with an analysis of the expressions 'creatio ex nihilo' and 'creation in the beginning'. He arrives at some determinants of specifically religious language, or, more precisely, of the specific qualities of the parabolic onlooks of the religious language of the Bible in contrast with secular, or, more exactly, purely constative language, and in contrast with a language which would permit only analogical onlooks. A religious onlook cannot specify the parabolic similarity which it establishes between the visible signs of God and the divine reality itself except in terms of the similarity between the appropriate attitudes. Secondly, it implies the recognition of a transcendent authority which demands an unlimited submission. In the third place, it implies the recognition by the believer of a divine and authoritative point of view (onlook) on which his own point of view (onlook) rests in its verdictive aspect. Finally, 'he believes that the onlook is self-verifying not merely because he himself makes it true as he lives in accordance with it, but primarily because a *hidden influence enables* him to act in accordance with it' (pp. 255-6).

This raises the fundamental question concerning the basis of religious onlooks. In Christianity this basis is Christ, 'the Exercitive, Verdictive and Commissive Word of God, the expression of God's glory, the victor of sin and darkness' (p. 265). None the less Christ does not 'provide an adequate basis for a self-involving confession of faith in God the Creator' (p. 267) except inasmuch as he is recognised as the most perfect manifestation of God's glory, as a living revelation, in his own person, of the mystery of God. And this recognition of Christ as the revealer of God is not possible outside a biblical context, outside the perspective of the onlooks proper to biblical language. 'For a Christian there is an intimate connexion between faith in Jesus Christ, as

the divine word, divine glory and divine saviour and faith
in the biblical Creator-God; these are bound up together in
a complex biblical onlook which is accepted and adopted in
a decision of faith' (p. 267).

2. QUESTIONS ARISING OUT OF EVANS' THEORY

Evans' subtle, profound and original analysis of self-involving
language allows for a new and far more precise formulation
of several traditional problems. From among the many
questions suggested by Evans, we shall concentrate on these
three: the nature of revelation, the possibility of speculative
theology and the nature of metaphysical propositions.

i. *The nature of revelation*
Evans demonstrates convincingly how linguistic analysis
can clarify the problem of the status of revelation. His
key-term in this context is SRB: soul-revealing behaviour,
which itself is to be understood in the light of the theory of
FRB—feeling-revealing behaviour. Just as an expressive
FRB reveals a sentiment and is in general a part of the
meaning of the interior sentiment which it reveals, so an
expressive SRB should be thought of as revealing a particular
quality of soul and by virtue of this it belongs to the meaning
of the term used to describe this quality. God does not show
himself in person but reveals himself through signs which
have the logical structure of an SRB: they reveal this or that
quality inherent in the divine reality and thus form part of
the meaning of the term which designates this divine quality
(e.g. the glory of God). This implies that one sign cannot be
replaced by another in the way that a purely informative
term can be replaced by another. The revealing sign is
analogous to the aesthetic expression of a state of soul. The
grasp of a given aesthetic expression brings an understanding
of the corresponding state of soul which is at once original
and irreducible to that which could be given by another
expression; there is no possible translation from one expres-

sion to the other. Similarly, a determinate revealing sign shows forth the divine reality in a particular way, so that, were this sign not available to us, our understanding of that reality would be different, and, conversely, no other sign could give us an identical understanding. Within the class of revelatory signs, however, there is one which is peculiarly privileged, namely, the person of Christ. Christ is the most perfect expression of the divine reality and as such is the norm for all other signs. It is because of their relation to him that the other signs are signs. In other words, all the revelatory signs other than Christ are themselves no more than figures of the unique and irreplaceable sign which is Christ.

If there is an analogy between the revealing sign and the expression of an interior state, then the conditions of understanding are the same in both cases. In order to understand the aesthetic expression, one must have a certain rapport with the interior state revealed in the expression. There is, in fact, a kind of resonance: the expression certainly opens the way to a new understanding, but only when it calls to a receptivity which is not purely passive—a receptivity which has, as it were, already a presentiment of the understanding towards which the expression points. Understanding is the actuation, in precise and concrete form, of a sensibility which is until then only a more general and abstract acquaintance of a certain domain of affectivity. Accordingly the revealing sign cannot be understood in its signification unless there is already a rapport between him who receives the sign and the divine reality which the sign reveals. To see in Christ the mystery of God, one must already possess a certain rapport with that mystery. One must already have been interiorly transformed by the divine action. And this is the circle characteristic of faith.

The analogy between aesthetic expression and revealing needs to be made more exact on this point. No doubt faith presupposes an openness which men can achieve only by a gift of God. Faith is itself a gift. The mystery of God when it calls to man creates in him a receptive field within which it can be welcomed. But the establishment of this receptivity presupposes its possibility, and this possibility has to be considered as a kind of predisposition, of presentiment, of waiting. The effective openness to the revealing signs (the active mood) which is the free gift of God, is based on the pre-existing possibility of openness (the passive mood) which belongs to the ontological structure of human existence. It seems, therefore, that we should distinguish two levels of rapport. There is active rapport, which is already faith, but considered from the side of the recipient, as openness to the mystery of God and to the understanding of the signs which reveal God. There is passive rapport, which is not yet faith but which constitutes in man an interior domain in which the revealing word may be heard and on whose foundation faith may open up. The analogy with aesthetic expression is valid only for passive rapport, because the possibility of aesthetic understanding belongs to the ontological structure of human being, it is not given in the aesthetic expression itself. The analogy cannot be extended to active rapport which supposes God's intervention, a gift, a transformation of soul. The revealing sign is not only the specifying form of an affective possibility. It is at once revelatory of a hidden reality and the establishment in the soul of the conditions for its understanding. Christ is the revelation of the mystery of God inasmuch as he is saviour; it is in this sense that he is the 'basis' of faith. He gives faith at the same time as he proposes himself to faith as its object, inasmuch as he is 'the mystery of God'.

ii. *The possibility of theology*

Evans' analysis is specifically concerned with biblical language, but it inevitably raises the question of the possibility of speculative theology. Biblical language, like religious language, is self-involving. Under what conditions, if at all, is it possible to institute a discourse on the content of faith which would remain within the perspective of systematic scientific enquiry? This is to raise the question of theology as science. If a theological science is possible, it would not seem to be so after the manner of an empirical science. No doubt theology is based on data, but these data must be considered not merely in their empirical reality, but as signs. Interpretation is called for, and the language of interpretation cannot be reduced to a purely constative language. Must it be considered as self-involving? Is it not rather the case that the projected theological science supposes the bracketing of precisely those religious attitudes which give biblical language its self-involving character? On the other hand, it seems that true theological understanding presupposes faith. What is at issue here is the distinction between properly religious language and the language of speculative theology. The issue could be couched equally well in terms of fundamental attitudes, of projects, as in terms of language. Perhaps there is an oblique usage of self-involving language? There would be a bracketing, but not a suppression, of the self-involving aspects. What is this bracketing? It is an effort to retain, as it were, laterally what is, for the moment, suspended like a presupposition necessarily present but not thematised as such. It is a methodological bracketing that is in question. It remains to be shown that such a tactic would allow for speculative discourse, the laying out of the internal logic of the context of revelation, and the recourse to philosophic categories in the explication of this content. This question is closely related to the following one to which we now turn.

iii. *The nature of metaphysical propositions*

What is to be said of properly philosophic—in the traditional sense—utterances? In this area the specific problems of theological discourse—the reference to faith and religious language—do not arise. None the less we must enquire whether or not philosophical discourse is purely constative. If this question is answered affirmatively, one must ask for the distinction, within the domain of constative utterances, between philosophic and scientific (i.e. empirical science) utterances. One may have recourse to analogy, but the analogy characteristic of philosophic utterance is not parabolic analogy; it is a speculative analogy based, not on similarity of attitude, but on the grasp of an intelligible relation of proportionality. Can such a grasp be expressed as a pure constative? Is there not in the invention of analogical concepts a specific intellectual activity which cannot be reduced to merely noting a relationship of fact and which is, accordingly, not purely constative? To undertake a logic of analogy, is it not necessary to take on oneself in some way the internal movement of the empirical reality so as to allow oneself be led along the articulations of its ontological structure and to grasp empirical appearance as the visible focus of a purely intelligible internal base? Is there not something in the philosophic enterprise which goes beyond empirical reality, beyond what is simply given, a revelatory breakthrough which, necessarily, is active and operative?

Have we not returned to self-involving language? and how is this to be distinguished from religious language? Unlike religious language, philosophic language does not include 'acknowledgement' as Evans calls it. It does include, however, an aspect of decision and commitment. By a specific intellectual decision one begins philosophic speculation. And access to the properly speculative domain presupposes the active grasp of the constitutive operations of the internal structure of reality. In this sense it presupposes commitment. Can we correctly speak of this commitment in terms of self-involving language in Evans' sense? The relevant presupposition does not seem the same as the presupposition in the sentence 'I put my trust in you, Lord'. In this sentence the commitment presupposed forms part of the meaning of the sentence and it is precisely this which constitutes its self-involving character. In a speculative utterance as such, one abstracts—in its meaning content— from whatever attitudinal presuppositions the utterance may be based on. It is worth noting that scientific discourse also is based on a decision, on the choice of a characteristic intellectual attitude. This presupposition, however, does not form part of the meaning of scientific utterances.

We are thrown back on our original question: precisely what is the difference between scientific (in the strict sense of empirical sciences) and philosophical utterances? Have we to allow, besides pure constatives and self-involving utterances, a third type of utterance arising from the speculative use of language? Or, within pure constatives, must we distinguish between empirical and speculative utterances? (This presupposes, clearly, that by 'pure constative' one does not mean a mere noting of the facts.) From the viewpoint of illocutionary force, it seems that one can classify into a single category all utterances arising from the basic project of critical and systematic knowledge—'science' is an older sense of that term. In Austin's classification, which Evans takes over, scientific language (in the broad sense) is a constative language. There remains the need to distinguish between the language of empirical science and the language of philosophy. If it is true that analogy is the characteristic of philosophic utterance, then our task must be the establishment of a logic of analogy. To this end the classical theory of analogy furnishes important clues. But the instruments of modern analysis allow for more rigorous developments and perhaps a deepening of traditional views.

V

Determinism and Responsibility:
The Language of Action

1. INTRODUCTION

In this chapter, within the general context of the problem of the interaction of determinism and responsibility, we raise the question of an adequate language to deal with specifically human action. More precision is required. We must take account of the immersion of human action in a network of determinism. On the one hand, there are available more and more precise analyses of the limiting conditions of human action, while, on the other hand, we are confronted with relative indeterminacy with respect to its orientation.

2. THE CONDITIONING FACTORS OF ACTION. PROCESSES AND STRUCTURES[1]

On the level of conditions we find a set of determinations which circumscribe the horizon of the possibility of action. Even if there is not strict determinism, there are certainly laws, that is, propositions expressing global regularities. At the same time, we must take into account a plasticity which makes human intervention possible. This intervention necessarily presupposes the interplay of nomological regularities and of plasticity.

[1]Ladrière uses the word 'architectures' perhaps because 'structures' has been pre-empted by a school. But 'architectures' would sound merely bizarre in English where only the derivatives are used in this sense, e.g., architectonic, with any frequency, although 'the architecture of matter' is acceptable. When 'architecture' is used in the translation here, it refers to the skill—*translator's note*.

It will be useful, if the level of human intervention is to
be situated exactly, to distinguish between processes and
structures. Processes are the regulated succession of states in
time. For a sequence of events to be a process and not
merely a chaotic juxtaposition there is required the intervention of rule, which is expressed in the laws governing the
process. These laws may be determinist or indeterminist. The
difference between them depends on how one defines state.
In the case of determinist laws, the state of a system is
defined by means of terms at once individual and direct. In
the case of indeterminist laws, the state of a system is defined
by means of a description in global or statistical terms. The
latter description is necessarily indirect; it does not cover
immediately whatever intervenes in a given process but refers
to the set of possibilities relative to what intervenes in the
process (for example the possible values of the speed of a
particle). The laws of the process may be called laws of
causality in that they express the link between states over
time. (The term 'causality' here means 'regularity'.) For
a contextual definition Hume's formula would serve:
'The same causes produce the same effects.' Lindsay and
Margenau offer a more precise version: 'The forces under
whose action processes occur do not vary over time.'[2] (For
example a force which depends on the inverse square of the
distance at an instant t cannot depend on the cube of the
distance at an instant t plus dt.)

Besides processes there are structures. The universe is
formed of organised sets disposed hierarchically. These sets
are organised according to laws. However, these laws do not
govern the succession of states but are laws of combination.
The appropriate language in their regard is not analysis but
algebra. It is true that processes intervene in the transition
from one configuration to another, but these processes are
different from those governing the succession of states. We
can contrast metamorphic with evolutive processes. An

[2]Cf. on this point R. B. Lindsay and H. Margenau, *The Foundations of Physics*,
London: Dover (Constable), 1957, 522.

evolutive process concerns the history of a system; a metamorphic process concerns the transformation of one system into another. The significant problem in the study of structures is that of the stability of configurations. Perhaps the goal of science is to invent a definitive explanation of structures in terms of processes, to reduce the laws governing configurations (in particular the laws of equilibrium) to the laws of processes (in the sense of evolutive processes). Statistical mechanics affords a good example of this type of reduction: it explains the macroscopic—configurational, therefore—properties of a system by relying uniquely on the properties of its elementary constituents and on the laws of motion governing these.

The human sciences teach us that there are configurations even in the domain of human behaviour. Let us use the term 'system' to designate an organised set—that is, a class of elementary constituents with determinate relations between themselves. The term can then apply equally well to a crystal as to a group. A system need not be absolutely rigid; it can be taken apart and put together again, it can be transformed into other systems. At least in part, the conditions of stability are determined by the properties of the environment. A modification of these entails a modification of the system. One can operate on the environment by employing the appropriate processes. The links between states and between constituents are not absolutely rigid, so most bodies are movable in space, energy can pass from one system to another, etc. What is of most interest to us here, however, is the fact that systems are not closed from above. From given systems, more complex systems can be constructed by using, for example, the property of mobility combined with given forces (like the force of gravity as in architecture), or by modifying the physical state of the constituents.

Our problem concerns the new possibilities opened up by transformation of this kind. Nor is the question trivial, for such transformations have a significant bearing on human

living (for example, atomic transmutation, genetic transformation, the toxic or therapeutic action of certain substances
on the nervous system etc.). But when we turn our attention
to the possibilities opened to action by the plasticity of its
conditioning factors, the question of the normative orientation of action inevitably emerges. According to what criteria
are the possibilities to be realised? More accurately, we have
to ask if these orientations can be analysed by the same
methods as the objective conditioning factors or if they can
be understood only in a different language. In other words:
does action fall under one or two forms of language?

3. SCIENTIFIC LANGUAGE

As a preliminary clarification we may examine the language
used in the analysis of the conditioning factors of action. It
is an extremely complex language including descriptive and
theoretic instruments. Scientific language may be divided
into two: an empirical and a theoretic part. The empirical
part allows for the description of perceptible reality (whatever is perceived directly or indirectly by means of
instruments). More precisely, it includes individual designa-
tions and observational predicates. As theoretic, the language
consists of a deductive system and interpretative rules, while
the deductive system itself is composed of a set of general
propositions and deductive rules. Such a system can be
formalised. It may be remarked that the deductive part of
the theory divides into a central and ancillary parts. The
central part is the body of hypotheses concerning the object
under investigation; the ancillary parts contain the theory
of measuring instruments used in the investigation. As for
the interpretative rules, they serve to establish a link between
the deductive system and the empirical part of the language.

A schematic description of how the language functions is
possible. A first move is the invention of hypotheses (this
move comes at the end of an exploratory phase which may
be extremely protracted). The application of deductive rules

to these hypotheses permits the second move: the derivation of propositions at a lower level of generality, which may be tested. A third move is the actual testing of these propositions. Thanks to the interpretative rules these propositions may be translated into propositions formulated in empirical terms, and so compared with the empirical propositions which express (at a certain level of generality) the results of observation. Testing may be considered as a process of either confirmation or corroboration. In the first case, the (eventual) agreement of the theoretic proposition with the facts is considered as strengthening its claim to truth. In the second case, this agreement is thought to set aside provisionally its falsification and so, in effect, to diminish its chance of falsehood.

4. THE PROBLEM OF NORMATIVE LANGUAGE

Is such a language apt to the study of the normative orientations of action? We are faced with evaluative utterances of the type 'This is good', 'This is preferable to that', 'This is not to be recommended', and with normative utterances of the type 'This is the rule to follow in such and such circumstances'. Can such utterances be put on the same footing as the utterances of scientific language? This question has been the object of the well-known discussion of the British school which led to the thesis on the fundamental difference between judgements of fact and judgements of value, between constative utterances and evaluative utterances.

It is worth briefly considering the development of the philosophy of language in the British school. At first, under the influence of the early Wittgenstein (of the *Tractatus Logico-philosophicus*), the fundamental problem is one of meaning and the criterion of meaning is placed in the existence of a method of verification. Later, under the influence of the later Wittgenstein (of the *Philosophical Investigations*), the criterion shifts: the meaning of a proposition is linked to its use. The relevant question no longer is: 'Is there a method of verification?' but 'Is there a way of using this proposition?' As there are many ways of using propositions, so there is a plurality of languages, each with its own logic. The distinction between judgements of fact and evaluative judgements must be understood within this perspective. For it is really a distinction between two forms of language.

Note that the distinction constative-evaluative is not the same as the distinction descriptive-nondescriptive proposed by the neo-positivists (Ayer or Carnap). The latter deny the descriptive character of ethical propositions. A descriptive proposition must be able to be true or false. It gives information and is formulated in the indicative mood. A normative proposition or an order is formulated in the imperative mood. The neo-positivists interpret these as either expressing the speaker's sentiments (like utterances expressing pleasure or pain) or as attempts to persuade the listener to act or feel in a certain way. The influence or persuasion is conceived, in this interpretation, as direct rather than as an indirect influence based on the communication of new information about the world.

It has been noted however that words with ethical meaning—whether verbs like 'ought' or predicates like 'good'—appear in propositions in the indicative mood, and that these propositions convey information (e.g. 'It is good that . . .'). Otherwise the neo-positivist arguments are predominantly negative: ethical propositions cannot be explained in naturalist terms and do not lend themselves to a verificatory procedure in the same way as informative propositions. Some authors have cast doubt on this argument. It is not certain that ethical propositions cannot be verified. According to these authors, ethical propositions have to be interpreted as descriptive propositions. But it is crucial to determine what it is that they describe. Two orientations can be discerned: some propose a naturalist interpretation, others a non-naturalist interpretation. In the first case, ethical propositions describe characteristics accessible to external observation or introspection. In the second case, they describe characteristics that are not accessible in this way, either directly or indirectly, like the harmony of life or the sublimity of conduct.

5. THE DISCOURSE OF DECISION

This brief glance at the controversies about the status of ethical propositions is no more than indicative of their history and may serve here merely as an introduction to an analysis of the languages of action. We come back to our original question: what precisely are the properties of action-language and how does it differ from scientific language? The latter is competent to analyse the conditioning factors of action. But how does it stand with respect to the characteristics proper to action as such? More precisely: how does it stand with respect to decision and responsibility?

Before tackling this question, it is worth noting that there are two kinds of proposition concerning decisions: propositions which are, or could be, formulated by whoever is making the decision; and theoretic propositions by means of which an attempt is made to account for the possibility and nature of decision in general.

We shall turn, first of all, to the subjective language of decision. Anyone making a decision can explain to himself or to others before making his decision, the considerations that he is taking into account. We find the following elements in his discourse:

(*a*) Constative judgements expressing the available information, which give a description of the situation.

(*b*) Propositions setting forth possible ways of action. These are not constatives but their status is comparable to scientific hypotheses. They permit the deduction of other propositions, less general in scope, which may be set against the propositions of the first type.

(*c*) Propositions—in the last analysis conjectural—expressing the consequences attendant on each of the proposed ways of acting. These propositions are deduced from those of the second group in the light of the first group by means of the rules of logic and mediated by the intervention of different theories (which may be probabilist in character). These propositions are, then, scientific in character.

(*d*) Evaluative propositions indicating to what extent the different outcomes envisaged as a result of the deductions already mentioned are to be recommended or condemned. These propositions are the result of applying some criterion of appreciation to the propositions of group (*c*). The application of a criterion to an envisaged situation cannot be compared with the explanation of a fact by means of hypotheses; in the latter case there is a deduction followed by an effective translation according to given interpretative rules, while in the former case a normative proposition is applied to a proposition expressing a possible state of affairs (therefore, a constative). Nor is it a question of deduction, for the normative proposition does not contain the particular cases which are precisely the issue in evaluative judgements. Since many norms may be invoked, there will be many sets of evaluative propositions, one for each norm.

(*e*) Normative propositions which mediate the evaluative propositions of the preceding group (*d*).

(*f*) A proposition expressing a preference for one of the normative propositions. This proposition must itself be based on a norm, and will, accordingly, have the status of an evaluative proposition—an evaluation of the second degree, as it were.

(*g*) A normative proposition expressing the norm by means of which the proposition (*f*) expressing preference may be formulated.

(*h*) A general maxim which can be formulated as follows: 'I shall choose the way of acting that will ensure the state of affairs most conformable to my preferred norm'.

Note here the introduction of the personal pronoun 'I'. The maxim (*h*) is a proposition in which the speaker risks himself; a proposition which, as it were, contains him and which expresses self-constraint. Recall in this connexion the performative utterances of Austin, e.g., utterances which realise what they express, like promises, thanks, or utterances which confer a function, title or name. Still, we must be careful that our proposition is formulated in the future tense—although it might also be expressed as a conditional: 'If I decide, my way of acting will be such as to ensure . . .' We may accord it, therefore, the status of a conditional performative.

(*i*) A proposition expressing the choice of a way of acting. This emerges very simply as a deduction from the general maxim above in conjunction with the propositions of the preceding group.

(*j*) Mediated by this deduction, the self-constraining nature of the general maxim (*h*) is transferred to the appropriate strategy S. This is expressed in the proposition: 'I propose the strategy S to myself' which is taken to mean 'I bind myself to the strategy S'.

(*k*) There is, finally, the following proposition: 'In binding myself to the strategy S, I accept in advance all the consequences, whether foreseeable or not, which result from my choice. I acknowledge in advance that these consequences will be imputed to my choice and that anyone has the right to designate me as the origin of these consequences'. Responsibility comes in, properly speaking, at this juncture, and the proposition may be labelled a 'responsibility-proposition'. Note again the personal pronoun 'I'. Further, the term 'anyone' in the second part of the proposition introduces another person. In the second part of the proposition, 'I' is introduced, so to speak, as the accused (in the accusative case—'me'). Responsibility is in fact a dialogic notion which implies the possibility of being subject to a trial whose purpose would be to determine to whom such or such a state of affairs should be attributed, to discover the source of this state of affairs, to find out at whose door the responsibility for the occurrence should be laid. A 'responsibility-proposition' has the status of a conditional performative, the form of a conditional commitment: 'I commit myself to plead guilty whenever my conduct is on trial'. (A more explicit expression of this would be: 'If I make a decision, and if later my conduct is on trial, I commit myself now to pleading guilty then'.)

These factors concern only the preliminaries of decision. The decision itself may be an interior act which, if expressed, can be formulated only by means of a performative, taking, for example, the form 'I decide to adopt this course of action'. This proposition makes effective both the self-constraining proposition and the responsibility-proposition, which were conditional performatives. The decision-proposition is a performative strictly so called. It expresses a modification of the speaking subject which does not come from outside, which is not the result of an interaction between subject and environment, which is not an event located in any objective process, but which is generated by the speaker's words. Naturally, a decision may be expressed in other ways, symbolically by a signature for instance, a gesture, a raised hand etc. But these symbols can always be translated into explicit language in the form of a decision-proposition.

Now if, after some time, the person who decides has to account for his decision he will use the above propositions except, of course, the decision-proposition itself. He can now speak of his decision only in retrospect, in the past tense, in the form of a constative: 'On such a day, I decided that . . .', which is equivalent to propositions used by historians. The 'I' is no longer significant and could be eliminated in favour of a third-person construction. The person who has decided could say of himself: 'On such a day, X decided that . . .'

Within the language of action, besides propositions belonging to scientific discourse, there are evaluative, normative and performative propositions. The first express preferences; the second express criteria and the third express actions. We must attempt to discover the relations between these different propositions and to understand why they occur together in the context of decision.

6. THE LANGUAGE OF THEORIES OF DECISION

With a view to the elucidation of that question we turn now to examine the theoretic effort to give an account of the possibility and nature of decision in general. We are no longer concerned with the person making a decision, but with the analyst of decision. His language will be theoretic and will be an effort to reconstruct a rationality and to rediscover an intelligibility supposedly at work in the act of decision itself. Can we not expect that this language will be scientific? After all, with respect to a decision already made, are we not in the position of the historian? We can produce a series of constatives and can attempt to explain the decision by inventing hypotheses about it. In most cases we shall not possess a detailed account of the actor's deliberations. We shall be forced to reconstruct this deliberation by discovering what the actor's situation was, by ourselves working out possible strategies in this situation, by imagining the criteria which the actor might have used—in other words, by making hypotheses about his values. Our judgements will not be normative but rather hypothetical propositions about normative judgements which could have expressed the actor's values. Once having formulated hypotheses of this kind we can check them by discovering if from them the decisions which have in fact been observed can be deduced. So far the movement is typically scientific.

Passing to a more generic viewpoint and leaving aside the historical concern to explain particular decisions we can endeavour to isolate the moves that occur in any decision whatsoever. We can attempt, for instance, a psychology of decision. Again the attempt is scientific: we must construct hypotheses concerning these moves and verify these hypotheses against concrete instances of decision, in appropriate circumstances (i.e., those which allow us as complete an analysis as possible of the situation and behaviour of the actor), endeavouring to control as well as possible the conditions under which the observation takes place. On the other hand it is possible, and we have sketched out the procedure, to work out the schema of propositions involved in decisions with a view to constructing a logic of decision emerging partly from formal logic and partly from the analysis of language. A study of this kind is meta-linguistic. Some writers call studies of this kind 'philosophy' but it may be argued that there is no significant difference between scientific language and meta-language. In any event a science tends at certain times to become meta-science. Meta-linguistic propositions are either analytic propositions and accordingly purely formal, or else constatives.

Nevertheless, none of these procedures yields an understanding of the systematic link which is apparent in the decision process between the value-judgements, the norms and the commitments of the actor. What precisely is the meaning of norms? How can they be established and justified? How are they used and what is their impact?

7. THE STATUS OF NORMS

A norm is not a fact. It does not express a state of affairs—even a possible or virtual state of affairs. Neither is it a hypothesis as this term is meant in the logic of science. It is not a general proposition from which we deduce particular propositions. A normative proposition permits the formulation of evaluative propositions. It does not operate as a premise in a deduction, nor is it on the same formal plane as its correlative evaluative proposition. With respect to the latter, it is on the meta-linguistic level, and is thus comparable to the rules of logic. A rule is not an axiom but a meta-theoretic proposition which makes deductions from propositions possible. But how is the norm itself justified? The rule is justified not from *a priori* general principles but *a posteriori* by its usefulness. A given system of rules is taken to be justified if it allows deductive expansion great enough to cover the domain of which we wish to speak. Thus, if we would speak of non-constructive mathematical entities, we would require a formal language using non-constructive rules (e.g. rules admitting an infinite number of premises). Is it possible to justify a norm of conduct in similar fashion? Such justification would have the following significance: the norm must be taken as justified by the consequences that flow from it in human conduct. In other words, it must be taken as justified if it gives rise to decisions that are useful, adequate or appropriate. One can hardly propose a justification of this kind without adverting to the question: useful, adequate or appropriate with respect to what? The terms mediating the justification of the norm are themselves normative. Accordingly, the attempt to justify a norm in the same way as a rule ends up in a vicious circle.

We may note at the same time that the allusion to the logical rule brings to light a norm which is immanent in scientific language but which, as such, does not belong to that language. It might be termed an adequation-norm which forces us to construct an analytic instrument proportionate to the domain to be explored. In fact this refers to a way of behaviour, an epistemological prescription, which is admitted to be sufficiently evident but which there is no great preoccupation to justify. It is not in any case a rule in the strict sense but a regulatory principle which arises from a different type of validating procedure. In the case of scientific language there is no circularity, but there is at one level a problem of normativity which confronts us once more with our difficulty: how are norms to be justified?

8. TRANSITION TO REFLEXIVE LANGUAGE

An examination of the connexion between normative and performative propositions may illuminate our way. In performatives the 'I' necessarily is included. In a performative the speaker performs an action of a certain kind on himself. This action is not merely linguistic but effects a transformation of the speaker. It has intersubjective import for the utterance belongs to others and becomes the source of a possible subsequent accusation. Now the speaker hazards himself precisely with respect to a norm. This is expressed in the conditional performative which expresses a link between subject and norm. It is in virtue of this link and on the basis of it that the decision proper emerges. This indicates that if the meaning of the norm and the principle of its justification are to be understood, and its rationality thus unveiled, then we must in some sense get to the inner core of this link, understand how and why it is constituted. But this implies the necessity of getting inside the subject himself by an attempt to come to terms with the subject no longer grammatically in the context of a proposition, but in his self-positing itself as act. In other words, we must go behind the expression to the act that subtends it. In a performative proposition, the grammatical subject expresses the subject of the act, but he is at the same time the object of this action inasmuch as he binds himself by it. The real structure of the performative is reflexive, even if not explicitly so. It may, of course, be explicitly reflexive as in the sentence 'I commit myself to returning this document'. The reflexive structure of the sentence expresses the subject's taking of a position which is truly self-positing, that is a putting of self into question, or again, it expresses an operation by which the subject affects himself. The self-positing of the subject is self-affecting.

It is this act of self-positing that analysis attempts to recover, and this demands a reflexive method—that is, a method consisting in moving back from expression to acts. What is involved here is not introspection, which is simply a description of inner facts, and which—ignoring for the moment the difficulties of public control—is expressed in a language that forms part of scientific language. Reflexion does not consist in a showing forth of facts, of events, or of objective processes. It is the theoretic effort through which thought tries to reconstitute an action; it is a process of constitution, not in its historical contingency, but in its essential law. It expresses itself in a discourse which would say explicitly what is hidden in the performative mode: the life of the speaking and deciding subject. Its concern is to delineate, not the individual aspects, but the general structure of that life. Yet it is precisely the general structure that is expressed in performatives. The 'I' of the 'I commit myself' is any 'I' whatsoever. The commissive proposition is the general form of each historical, personal, concrete commitment. The function of the grammatical 'I' is to provide the speaker with a sort of anchorage, to allow him to take on, himself, language and its speaking, by identifying his own contingent and particular life with the universal life of language. For this reason language can reveal acts. Under the general forms of language the general form of constituting life is expressed. And this constituting life operates in every 'ego' precisely that which posits it as 'ego'.

9. CONCERNING THE PRINCIPLE OF JUSTIFICATION OF NORMS

The mode of discourse in which decision at once expresses and projects itself shows that in decision the subject takes up a position with respect to himself, binds himself, goes beyond his temporality in order to affect himself in a still non-existent future. This self-finding is neither arbitrary nor whimsical but operates under normative control. Taking up a position is the assumption and ratification of a norm which thus ceases to be an external principle and becomes the vital thread of particular behaviour. In itself the norm is general. In decision the subject makes it his own without depriving it of its virtually universal signification. It is true that there is no universal agreement concerning norms. Some authors have suggested that they be considered as hypotheses in relation to conduct which could be justified by their consequences. The lack of agreement is put down to the difficulties inherent in verification. But if an appeal to verification is to be made, this cannot be conceived except in terms which are themselves normative: satisfaction, goodness, the sublimity of a state of conscience. And we are back within the circle. The supposed universality of the norm is not, then, of the same character as that of the scientific hypothesis. Yet it is real. Even when there is not agreement in fact, there is the continuing search for agreement. Everyone tries to justify his norms to others and intends, through the norm which he effectively invokes, a norm really universal and unique, which would not be merely formal but the precise indication of a content, a concrete universal. The universality of the norm signifies not an already achieved intersubjective agreement, but the intention, intrinsic to it, of that supremely real norm which is, in a sense, already operative within the norms invoked in the present but which, in another sense, is always in the future.

How can the subject take up a position with respect to the norm? Where does the norm come from in the last analysis? It might be suggested that it is simply the reflexive taking up of determinations immanent in objective reality. On this tack one would come back to a wholly scientific explanation, for these determinations have to be accessible to scientific analysis. It seems certain that the study of systems, particularly of complex systems, will reveal some finalities. Of course, in every system there is an internal finality inasmuch as there is priority of the whole with respect to the parts. No particularly valuable indication can be gleaned from this finality in which the system is not transcended. However, the existence of evolutionary movements from system to system seems to indicate a finality of derivation, a directional finality. In this connexion one might speak of a general law of universalisation.

Even accepting this, these indications do not give us norms. If the criteria of action do nothing but take up (whether consciously or not) the finalistic tendencies of nature (including, of course, nature in ourselves), then the problem of transforming these indications into norms remains. A nomological proposition is not to be confused with a normative one. The existence of such indications—if they may be admitted as seems allowable—would be valuable in that they could serve as the material of criteria; they would allow us, as it were, to anchor our decision in a tangible substructure which would give them their effectiveness. But the mysterious and yet essential moment is the metamorphosis of a natural solicitation, nomological as it may be, into a normative inspiration. There is a position taken with respect to natural finalities. What exactly is this taking of a position?

Can an ideal finality be invoked? But where is it to be found? Is there a good in itself, the demands of which are merely expressed in normative principles? Then how would we have access to this good in itself? Can we fall back on an axiological intuition? And even supposing this were possible, would it suffice as a base for norms in their particularity? And how would one explain the lack of universal agreement, the uncertainty and the fragility of norms? Or would an intuition of this sort be so general as to yield nothing but an empty form instead of the content and the principle of intersubjective verification which it should give? Doubtless whenever we refer to norms, no matter how diverse or contradictory they may be, we can fall back on the notion of value contained in them. But value is a pure form. In fact, the formal aspect of value does no more than express, and quite inadequately at that, the normativity of the norm.

If we cannot fall back in the last analysis on either a natural or an ideal finality, what is left besides the self? But if we construct a hypothesis making the self the source of the normativity of norms we must avoid representing the self as given in advance within an *a priori* system of norms which reflexion can reveal. The common uncertainty with respect to norms reflects their non-*a priori* character. What we are calling a 'norm' is none other than the particular, contingent, historical formulation of an exigence which is at once radical and without content. Man is a natural being and, as such, subject to all the forms of determinism described by the sciences. He is constructed of elementary particles, molecules, cells and there is no reason to suppose that these elements cease to obey their own laws whenever they happen to come together in a human body. However, the study of human events, especially expressive events, indicates that man is something other than merely natural. Cultural systems reveal a finality that goes beyond the natural finality, whether holistic or directional, proper to systems in general. Of the former one could say that it is a dominance; a dominance which is pure affirmation—that is, the word itself. Yet the word is always enigmatic. Man remains a puzzle to himself not so much as regards knowledge but as regards action. The appeal to a norm constitutes the distance between natural being and the enigmatic being of man.

10.   HUMAN RESPONSIBILITY AND ETHICAL DISCOURSE

To say that man is enigmatic in practice is to say that he is called to discover himself progressively in his acts, that he is called to put himself continually to the test. Always situated, he must always overcome the situation. His situation is his natural being, his insertion in the cosmos and whatever his past actions have made of him. Every situation repeats the enigma. Each situation calls for him to speak himself, to overcome himself in his response to the ever recurring question: what is man? In his reply, throughout time, man discovers himself and the norms he formulates are but the historic traces of his previous answers. Thus the properly human being of man—which constitutes him as an 'ego'—is twofold. On the one hand it is wholly in the future, held in suspense, as it were, delayed. On the other hand, it is already present as the exigence of man to face himself, as the strength of which the ego partakes over against the questions which confront it, as the place in which its being, held in suspense, occurs. The relation of the present self to the self to come is not an analytic relation: the future is not contained in the present for the future is not simply the unfolding of the present. The future ego is not a content, a summation but an emergent quality. The decision is true because it constructs the future, because it introduces the determination of act into the indetermination of question.

Here we reach the essence of responsibility. Man is responsible for himself in so far as he is an egological being. He is responsible before himself. The present self must answer, at every instant, for what it presently is before the future self which is at once the present self's future and judge, always present with it on its perilous way. Beneath the norm there is, then, the ego's discovery of itself, that is the slow emergence of the affirmation of the human in man. From time to time, in privileged individuals, inspired perhaps or helped by a higher power, the possibilities of ethical perfection are revealed. But in its totality, obscurely, through many detours and deceptive corridors humanity advances towards what Kant called the city of ends. Perhaps only grace can open its gates.

If a norm is never more than the codification of a moral invention then it is never adequate. In every situation there is something new. Each occasion is, in a way, a new beginning. So from normative to evaluative judgement there is not an analytical transition. The normative judgement corresponds to the history of moral experience, the evaluative judgement to its present. In both there is an anticipation of the future—that is, the expression of an exigence which calls us from the infinity of our future and sets us in our own place; from there we can be made to say what our being truly is, and made to answer for that which, by reason of our constitution, we must answer for. The self-positing of the subject is the continuously renewed assertion of it: the ever uncertain yet sovereign face of man in us. Faith tells us what it is: the image of God in ourselves.

In action man risks, tests, constructs himself. Ethical discourse, which is the effort to understand and justify action as such, both prolongs and advances action. For it is itself action. In it the self discovers and articulates itself. It is the effort to translate into the finitude of a word of a day's duration the infinity of a call which comes from beyond all days and announces the mystery of which our lives are the patient unravelling.

VI

Science, Philosophy and Faith

I. INTRODUCTION

It has become commonplace to speak of the 'scientific mentality', and of how difficult it is for one endowed with it to have a true understanding of the experience of faith. Now, in so far as science is not only a mode of knowing but also an attitude of mind, and conversely, in so far as faith is not only an attitude of mind but also a mode of knowing, the question arises of the relation between the two forms of experience. And in so far as philosophy claims to furnish explanations of the ultimate determinants of human existence and so links—at least in appearance—with the dimensions of faith, the question arises of the relation between philosophy and faith. Finally, in so far as science and philosophy both lay claim to being in possession of a methodology of truth, the question arises of the relation between them.

Some light may be shed on these questions by our taking up an existential point of view and envisaging science, philosophy and faith as global movements in which a man engages himself totally (although in differing modalities) and through which he attempts to constitute his relations with the world and himself. But it will also be useful to bracket the role of the fundamental attitudes which give to these different movements of the spirit their respective characters, and to consider them uniquely as knowledge. No doubt this is an abstraction but it may none the less be useful since often what is called a conflict of mentalities is nothing more than an apparent conflict between modes of knowledge and the result of methodological confusion. Sometimes the confusion springs from an imperialism regarding criteria of truth which would, in all domains and in every situation, apply that which is legitimate and fruitful only in the domain of the empirically verifiable. More frequently no doubt the confusion arises from a too precipitous desire for unity and synthesis, whether one hopes to extrapolate from the methods and concepts that serve one of its sectors to the whole of experience, or whether one's aim is to bring together in the unity of a 'vision' all the orders of truth. The desire for synthesis is legitimate and fruitful, but slowly and piecemeal we discover that the synthesis is not to be in the order of representation, that it is eschatological and consequently the object of hope, not demonstration. The path of synthesis passes by the recognition of the plurality of orders.

2. THE CRITICAL REQUIREMENT

Science and philosophy are both specifications of the idea of rational knowledge. In both we find the unfolding of a knowing that is not only knowledge of the world but of itself, that not only grasps a content but also includes a justification of its product. In other words, in both cases there is a critique—knowledge operating on itself. The critical demand appears first of all in a negative form: it is a questioning of evidence, and as such it demands that the immediate knowledge of natural experience of the world be replaced by a knowledge mediated by a reductive operation. The exposure of the fallacious character of evidence cannot signify the suspension of all forms of evidence; this would involve the renunciation of all forms of givenness, which would be acceptable only if knowledge were conceived as a work of pure imagination. But, leaving aside for the moment the existence of absolutely imaginary creation, it would seem impossible to justify an undertaking of imaginary knowledge as soon as one severs all link with some exterior form of control. The real problem of the critique of evidence, then, consists in practising an appropriate bracketing and thus joining with privileged kinds of evidence. The task is to discover the procedures of reduction which will bring us to data at once controllable and fertile—that is, to data which furnish the means of their verification and which also include indications of other data and so open the field to a systematic exploration of the link between data.

This brings us to a second and positive aspect of the critical demand: the desire for system. Reduction to privileged evidence should not be considered except as a preliminary to the critical demand: it is the condition of a reconstitution of reality which would be in principle exhaustive. Such a reconstitution is evidently not a simple return to immediate data which have been subjected to reductive critique; it is not merely a matter of reconstructing the given by means of elements that have been isolated. The function of the reduction is to make possible the substitution of the immediate datum by a purely intelligible organism by means of which this datum will be understood in its truth. The transformation of the datum into its truth, which is the goal of the critical movement, is realised in the construction of a system. What constitutes the system as system is the link understood not in the sense of a fortuitous connexion but in the sense of a necessary concatenation. The interrogation of reduced data according to their linkages is only a propaedeutic to the construction of a purely intelligible system of linkages. Such a system in principle aims at completeness. And this for two reasons. On the one hand, the power of the system—exactly what is demanded of it—is to manifest exhaustively the signification of the integrated elements; and this signification accrues to each element in its relations with others and it is not exhaustively understood until the totality of its relations is exhibited. On the other hand, the system does not show the necessity of the relations it develops except in so far as it describes the complete circle of relations and so illustrates the fact that whatever point one starts from one can reach any other point. And this condition can be fulfilled only in so far as the system is closed. The idea of system manifests a third aspect of the critical demand: method. Nothing allows us to determine in advance how the governing idea of critical knowledge will fulfil itself. At its point of departure the exigence which defines such knowledge is pure exigence, indeterminate orientation, empty anticipation, purely formal willing. It can develop itself only by determining itself, but it cannot determine itself except from itself. In its initiation it must discover the manner of its unfolding. Now the critical demand cannot be content with mere groupings and disordered essays, it cannot leave itself to chance and the favours of the gods for the revelation of what it seeks. It is not critique except in so far as it controls its own efforts and organises them according to norms issuing from its own essence. Method is precisely this determination of the critical exigence by itself which allows it to replace the vague original intentions by a strategy defined by precise and rigorous plans.

Because method is not given *a priori* its elaboration is inseparable from its unfolding. In other words the method is necessarily steeped in historicity. And the historical experience of the constitution of method has taught us that the way is neither simple nor unique. Nor is it any way privileged. Far from effecting the convergence of attempts towards the elaboration of a progressively unified strategy, method has proliferated. If some methods seem more established and better proven still none can be considered as universal models to which progressively every effort should conform. The attempt to invent method leads to the discovery of the plurality of methods. If methods are diverse, they are not, for all that, equivalent. The goal is total intelligibility which for us is expressed in system, but there is more than one way of understanding system and each modality of system reveals an appropriate aspect of the intelligibility of the real. To recall only the greatest and clearest differentiations, there is the differentiation—in fact

very old but only recently understood in any way fully—
between (positive) science and philosophy, the differentiation, again early, between formal science and the sciences of
the real, and finally the very recent differentiation between
the empirico-deductive sciences and the hermeneutic
sciences.

3. THE DOMAIN OF FORMALISM

Precisely in so far as it was the science of method, logic was,
for a long time, considered apart from the other sciences.
It was thought to precede the other sciences and to prescribe
the modalities of their attempts. The idea of logic was the
idea of a universal canon of reason. Today logic has become
enormously complexified; at the same time it has ceded its
privileged position (which was in any case a sort of privilege
of principle). But it has gained in efficacity. Rather than
speak of logic one may speak of the investigation of foundations. The goal of this investigation is not to determine in
advance the procedures of science—as if the scientific
enterprise were merely the actuation of preconceived plans
—but to determine the exact status of the fundamental
concepts and procedures of contemporary science and to
provide them with as exact and rigorous a critical basis as
possible. The most general foundational problems are
philosophic—e.g. those concerning the nature of method,
logic, truth. But there is a vast category of problems that
belong to science proper. Today each science has its
corresponding foundational enquiry. Sometimes these are
distinguished as in the case of mathematics and meta-
mathematics. Sometimes the distinction remains implicit as
is the case with many aspects of theoretical physics which
emerge in fact from a veritable 'metaphysic'. Furthermore,
formal logic, by adopting the methods of mathematics, has
become extraordinarily diversified and has finally been
transformed into a general science of formal systems which
it seems less and less possible to distinguish from mathematics (in the traditional sense of the term). The methods

9

of this science have proved to be very fertile as the case of meta-mathematics (admittedly a privileged example) illustrates. The multiplication of logical systems—that is, of pure deductive systems, on the one hand, and the great development of mathematics, on the other, when linked with their move to a very high level of abstraction, reveal the field of the formal with an unprecedented clarity.

At first sight, the domain of pure formalism seems essentially characterised by deduction. It is true that deductive systems provide the clearest and, so to speak, the most 'classical' examples of formal systems. But the deduction itself appears only as a particular solution to a general problem which is to provide precise criteria allowing the isolation of a privileged sub-set of propositions from within a given set. The propositions of the sub-set are characterised as 'true' or simply as 'theorems' of the theory in question. In a deductive system the procedure used to isolate 'true' propositions consists of giving a list of propositions accepted at once as true, the axioms of the system, and a set of rules which permits one to move from one or several 'true' propositions to other 'true' propositions. By means of the given axioms and rules it is possible to generate progressively the complete set of true propositions from an already completely described sub-set, namely the axioms. There are other means of isolating the 'true' propositions of a theory —e.g., a semantic method by which one associated with every proposition of the theory, by means of rules formulated recurrently, the predicates 'true' or 'false'.

Whatever the procedure, what is essential is the nature of the criteria used to formulate the rules (whether deductive or semantic rules). The criteria must be such that the application of these rules avoids all ambiguity. A formalism constitutes a 'domain of truth' characterised by strict and complete rules which allow one to determine without ambiguity whether or not a proposition belongs to the domain, by a step-by-step process—that is, beginning from the elementary constituents, moving through the more complex constituents until finally one reaches the proposition itself no matter how complex.

When one persists in the investigation of the exact nature of the criteria which are involved in formal rules, one notes that the steps which subtend the formal manipulations and can be considered as truly foundational with respect to known formalisms are probably purely combinatory. If this is the case it means that the essence of formalism is combinatory. The intelligibility proper to the formal is revealed, and this has been studied in 'combinatory logic'. This logic deals with operators, which are entities of the second degree as it were, for by definition operators deal with objects, which can themselves be operators but in so far as they fall under the action of an operator must be treated as arguments of that operator. The operators envisaged by combinatory logic are relatively simple: e.g., the operator of inversion which changes the order of two objects, the group operator which isolates two objects in a given series and applies the first to the second as a function of its argument. The concern then is with pure operations, considered in themselves and abstracting from kinds of objects on which they operate. The concern also is with operations that can be effectively realised, under the constant control of intuition, by using an appropriate algorithm. So we come back to the old idea of the calculus but at a level of abstraction and generality so that we reach at once the foundations of the formalist method.

At the centre of the calculus is the operation. At the level of pure combinatory theory, objects disappear and one is left with an empty scheme of effectuation as such. Of course for the operation to be effected in fact, there must be objects on which to operate; or, at least, it must be clear how objects are to be operated on. Generalising from a method originating in algebra, formalism provides quasi-objects in the form of indeterminates. Their nature is not further determined. Their role is simply to serve as supports for the operations studied. Their meaning is exhausted, so to speak, in this function. By operating in the void in this way formalism manifests in an abstract state the operative power of the operation. In this way the realm of the operation becomes intelligible. The comprehension of the operation is rigorously contemporaneous with its effectuation. There is not a pre-given essence of which the effectuation of the operation is merely the concrete transcription. There is no intuition of meaning controlling operative practice. There are no general principles of which the algorithms are merely applications. The operators may be described in a non-formal way, they can be characterised by indicating their effects. But the only strict definition of an operator is formal: it consists in giving the algorithmic scheme of its workings. And the only way of truly understanding the nature of the operator is by manipulating the schema, that is by effecting concretely the transformations, the rules of which are given by the schema.

There is here an intuition, one might say, in the sense that the application of schemas is accompanied at all times by a direct grasp of the nature of the acts performed. These acts are of great simplicity and they are immediately understandable because they are translated by concrete manipulations, by entirely effective scripts that a machine could perform as well. Of course the scripts and the movements of the machine are only the visible transcription of the acts. But it belongs to the nature of the latter that they can be adequately understood in these sensible transpositions. Thus, if there is an intuition it is not a global intuition which would grasp in one sweep the whole intelligible content of the operation, but an analytic intuition which deals with one aspect at a time, with the partial moments of an operation which will be understood as a whole only at the end of the process. This elementary intuition is pragmatic: it is only vision in so far as there is effective action in the empty field of the pure forms of the calculus. Vision and action are inseparable, they cover each other exactly, because the action is entirely transparent. The reason why this is possible is that one is not dealing with real action in the world and so the action is not affected by the contingence, the unforeseeableness, the opacity, of the real world.

The isolated operation, however, is still purely a medium. If it is true that some formal disciplines expressly concern fundamental operations and their properties and thus permit an increasingly exact comprehension of the formalising procedures, still the formal domain is not to be reduced to a mere operative game. In a sense the operation is the material of which the formalism is made. But the formalism must itself be understood as a system. The goal of combinatory analysis is to reconstitute, from the most elementary operations possible, the more complex operations immanent in the most diverse formal enquiries and so gradually to elucidate the mechanisms permitting formal construction in general. In the present state of knowledge we do not possess a single system in which all the known mathematico-formal disciplines might be placed. On the contrary, we have an enormous multiplicity of systems. But the fact that it is possible to move between the systems leads one to believe that they all belong to the same order of reality. Even if it is not possible some day to construct a comprehensive system which would concretely manifest the unity of the formal, we may still consider this unity as an immanent condition of the (partial) systems so far constituted. The systems already developed constitute limited results in a field which seems infinite and which—as opposed to existing formalisms that represent only part of the possibilities of formalisation and are, in consequence, relative—may be named the absolute formal field.

This field is the locus of operations. In so far as it is absolute it represents the presumptive totality to which all the operative practices belong by right. We cannot represent this in an actual form, for such a representation would have to be a total system and the possibility of constructing a total system is outside our present horizon and is, perhaps, non-existent. But our experience of the formal, through the knowledge we have of existing systems, reveals it to us as a domain of apparently limitless possibilities. It is precisely this anticipation of possible formalisations that we conceive under the form of an absolute field. Since it offers to operation a locus of realisation that is never exhausted it constitutes a privileged domain of intelligibility. In so far as it represents the presumptive unity of all formal constructions it constitutes a closed area—that is, it corresponds to a totality of intelligibility. And it is this totality which all the formal disciplines, in their different manners, intend. All modes of formal construction, whether the diverse modalities of speculation on pure space, variations on the fundamental laws of composition or of the pure combinatory theory, are merely concrete approaches to a sort of commanding construction which would be the integral of all effectable constructions and of the pure possibility of construction in general. The intelligibility of the construction is not complete intelligibility although it is oriented towards its own totalisation. It constitutes nonetheless a sort of extreme realisation of the demand for intelligibility.

As has been suggested already in the case of the combinatory theory, formal intelligibility may be characterised by its transparence, or again by an absence of residue. Very simply—and very traditionally—formal thought is exact thought. This means that it perfectly coincides with its object, that it gives an adequate comprehension of it, or—what amounts to the same thing—that it perfectly controls itself and in a sense reduplicates itself entirely in the act of its effectuation. The reason for this is that it is its own object. What characterises the formal is precisely the bracketing of objects and the realisation (in the sense of 'to become real', 'to become substance') of the operation, or the construction. Note that the formal domain is not limited to strictly finite constructions nor even to effective constructions but that it extends, as the example of non-constructive mathematics proves, to the representation of non-effective constructions. The acts by means of which these constructions are defined and analysed are themselves operative and as such must answer to defined conditions of effectivity. There is then an inescapable anchoring of the formal in effectivity, but it is possible to think effectively the non-effective and so the formal domain cannot be confined to the basic constructions which are themselves characterised by effectivity. But whether it is a question of effective or non-effective operators, it is always of operators. The formal domain is that of pure thought. And the domain of pure thought is that of operations: pure thought is thought of itself, not in the sense of reflexive philosophy, nor in the sense of a grasp of the positing activity as such by itself, but in the sense of operative activity—that is, of the effecting of pure relational schemas. Pure thought is thought of itself because it is nothing else than the understanding of the diverse modes of concatenation and of transformation in which the operative praxis is resolved and because this understanding takes place precisely in the form of operative activity which grasps itself by effecting itself.

In so far as pure thought is abstracted from all objects and in so far as it elicits no other intuition than the intuition of algorithmic activities, it may be termed *a priori*. As *a priori* it has, so to say, a demiurgic quality for it unfolds the set of all constructional possibilities in the totality which it is. Intending its own totalisation it grasps the particular relational forms as moments in a universal structure of all possible relations—that is, as elements in a total virtual system. The step which leads it towards the progressive actualisation of this virtual horizon is a step towards the concrete. And this in two senses. Firstly, the total formal system, if it could be constructed, would be, in relation to the partial systems, in the relation of concrete to abstract: concrete in that it would reveal the totality of possible constructions (among which, each one on its own remains partial and, as isolated, is abstract) and would effect simultaneously all conceivable connexions. The move to totality would be at the same time, and necessarily, closure, and the latter would be a move to existence: in the total system, the formal field, which remains for us merely the indications of a system of virtualities, would become real, would enter so to speak into a visible body of effectuation. Secondly, the total system, in so far as it would provide the representations of all possible modes of construction in their necessary connexions and so in their unity, in so far as it would thus reach the fullness of logical existence, would appear as immediate possibility of realisation and so as imminence of physical existence. In so far as it reached the fullness of formal representation and in this sense became a completed formal structure, a concrete logical structure, it would appear as calling for its application to the level of real effectivity—that is, in a domain of objects, or as calling for its immersion in the phenomenal field of 'physis'. As the domain of the appearance of pure formality—i.e. of the operations as such—logic reveals the ontological connexion linking it with physics. It exhibits that which in itself goes beyond pure logic; it evidences the *a priori* framework of the world, as knowledge of the world of forms of which the real world is at once the support, the visible transposition and the truth.

4. THE NATURAL SCIENCES

We are now in a position to understand how the recourse to formal knowledge appeared very early to be the key to a rigorous knowledge of nature. Since the formal domain is a privileged locus of intelligibility, the project of the knowledge of nature in the light of that intelligibility seemed very natural. But how was this project to be effected? We do not possess the total system of formal determinations. We have only fragmentary systems whose relations we know badly and whose place in the complete formal field we do not know at all. How can we benefit from the clarity proper to these systems in our constitution of a science of the real world? The historical resolution of this problem, at least with respect to inanimate nature, is well known. A formal system as such yields knowledge without content. For a formalism to be used as an instrument for the understanding of a content—that is, for it to be applied to knowledge founded in data, we must add to the formalism such rules of interpretation as will establish a precise correspondence between the propositions of the formal system and the empirical affirmations in which we express our knowledge of the data.

The interpretative rules thus mediate between the domain of pure formality and that of empirical determinations. Such a mediation cannot be established unless there is a certain homogeneity between the terms to be related. It will, accordingly, be necessary to establish this homogeneity and to that end two tasks have to be undertaken.

First, there is the choice of an appropriate formalism. This is made by casting about among the known formal disciplines for the elements which seem most appropriate to the proposed end—that is, those elements which seem most closely related to the type of phenomenon under discussion. (Thus, in the investigation of oscillatory phenomena recourse to periodic function appears quasi-natural.) Certainly there can be no question of relying on any principle *a priori*. Certainly, too, guide lines will not in general be lacking—analogy, generalisation, care to preserve certain fundamental principles as principles of invariance and conservation. But in the final analysis a sort of divination is required in the choice of a suitable formalism and there is no guarantee that this or that choice is the best possible. Advance is by trial and error and one must be ready to judge of the appropriateness of the choice—and willing to make different attempts if need be.

Secondly, there is the adaptation of the reality studied to the type of language provided by the formalism. This means that suitable abstractions within the reality must be provided for, the bracketing of certain aspects of the reality that do not apparently lend themselves to formal representation and the retention of those aspects only that do seem susceptible of such representation. Thus in the early stages of modern physics the famous distinction between primary and secondary qualities was introduced with a view to making possible the application of geometric analysis to physical reality. The reduction of phenomena to their quantitative aspects and the theory of measurement, which is almost a corollary of this reduction, occur within this context. The strict definition of the measuring procedures allows the setting up of non-ambiguous rules of correspondence between formal and empirical language.

But recourse to measurement, at least in the classical sense, where measurement consists in the co-ordination of a phenomenally manifested, physical magnitude to a rational number, is required only when the formal instrument used is the language of the theory of functions.

It is certainly natural enough to avail of this theory when there is question of showing the mutual interdependence between diverse physical magnitudes, for example between space and time, between temperature and pressure. Still there is no *a priori* limitation to this type of formalism. Note that contemporary physics has recourse to a considerably more extended theoretic language in which purely relational notions (e.g. symmetry) play a very much more important role than metric notions. At all events a certain idealisation of phenomenal reality is necessary. Physics speaks about the phenomenal world but in an indirect way through the mesh of schematic representations which provide for the formal operations a domain of appropriate objects and of which the phenomenal world is in a way only the distant and forgotten support.

Once the choice of a suitable formalism has been made and the appropriate level of abstraction fixed, correspondence rules can be precisely formulated and it is then possible to reason about the phenomenal reality (or rather about its abstract schema as it is presented in experimentation) within the framework of that formalism. Explanation will then consist in reconstituting as it were *a priori* the phenomenon under investigation. The explanatory schema can be set out more precisely as follows: what has to be explained is how such a real system manifests such phenomena—more precisely, how it passes from one state, considered as the initial state, to another. Information on these topics will be expressed in empirical propositions. Thanks to the correspondence rules these propositions may be translated into theoretic propositions which will be added to the true propositions of the theory—that is, of the formal system. The next move is to determine by virtue of the theory alone the subsequent evolution of the phenomenal system under consideration. To this end it is essential to deduce from the set of true propositions of the theory (i.e. from the fundamental principles of the theory plus the propositions describing the initial state of the system) a proposition describing the state of the system to be explained. Finally, this proposition can be translated by way of the correspondence rules into an empirical proposition corresponding to possible observations. If the proposition so obtained corresponds to the observed state, then one has an explanation of that state.

Since there is no advance guarantee that the selected formal system is apt for a study of the phenomenal domain in question, the question of the adequacy of the formal system (that is, the theory) to the domain will be a constant preoccupation of the investigator. To assure this adequacy within the relatively stringent limits indicated by the practice of science, recourse must be had to verification (or falsification), the mechanism of which is extremely complicated if it is examined in detail. An important reason for this complexity is the fact that in general the interpretation of observations is not immediate but demands the introduction of theories other than the one to be proved. Thus the verification process introduces many theories at once and it is difficult to isolate the role of the theory to be proved. However, if verification is reduced to its most essential aspects, it follows a schema parallel to that of explanation.

Our interest at present, however, is not the verification of theories but their explanatory power. The mechanism of explanation, as we have seen, consists in bringing to the concrete phenomenon the intelligible force of formal manipulations. Essential to explanation is deduction. With deduction we are once more in the domain of operations and in a general way, with the formal field. In the empirico-deductive sciences the essential step is the introduction (by way of the interpretative rules whose decisive importance is thus manifest) of real objects, belonging to 'physis', into the pure formal field. The possibility of this rests on the fact that pure formalism includes quasi-objects which operators act upon in the void. These quasi-objects may be interpreted as taking the place of possible objects. It is possible to capitalise on the proper intelligibility of the operations by replacing the quasi-objects of the formalism by real objects (or, more exactly, their formal representations), or—and this comes to the same thing—by making the quasi-objects (by a sort of convention incorporated in the interpretative rules) play the role of phenomenal objects. By thus explaining the phenomena of the real world within a formal theoretic framework, we substitute for the real operations by which the phenomena are mutually conditioned and recipro-cally determine the modalities of their appearance, the unreal or purely virtual operations of the formalism. In themselves the former are inaccessible for at the level of empirical observations we have only their results. The latter, on the other hand, are in a sense connatural; we understand them through and through because we ourselves realise them.

The conditions under which theories are elaborated are such that we never know exactly the extent to which our theories correspond to the actual course of the world. We know, when a theory resists verification, that there are some common points between the theory's formal apparatus and the unfolding of phenomena. But these common points are relatively few in number in comparison with the range of phenomena and verifications that are in principle possible.

Further, they have only a punctual character and give us no assurance of any correspondence in the zones lying between the points. Also the practice of the empirico-formal sciences forces us to abandon the picture idea of truth. To the extent that a theory survives its verification it gains a certain weight, but this by no means signifies that it produces a sort of representative double of reality. We interrogate reality as it comes to us through the schematic manifestations of empirical science by using intellectual instruments borrowed from the formal domain. But the formal concepts are not to be regarded either as the result of an induction from phenomenal data or as the translation of an intellectual intuition which would give *a priori* the key to phenomena. Neither strict empiricism nor classical intellectualism seems to be able to give a satisfactory account of the role of theories in the empirico-formal sciences. The real epistemological problem posed by these sciences seems to lie in the exact nature of the formal and in the relation uniting pure formalism to the physical world. It behoves us to see this relation not *a posteriori*, relying on the experience of science, but *a priori*, basing ourselves on the grasp of the nature of the formal as such.

Whatever the case, it seems that the mode of intelligibility proper to the empirico-formal sciences must be related to the mode of intelligibility proper to the purely formal sciences, that is to the intelligibility of the operations. However, while in the purely formal sciences the operations are effected in the void, in the empirico-formal sciences they are so interpreted as to appear as 'representatives', provisionally accepted as valid, of the internal operations of the 'physis'. We understand nature by attempting to mime its operations in our own fashion, by re-enacting for ourselves the unfolding of the phenomena whose traces we note. In reality our explanations are productive; our theories produce what nature produces; they allow us to reconstitute in the abstract, with analogical models, the concrete concatenation of real phenomena.

There is no question but that this way of approaching reality and of tracing the outline of its truth presupposes a fore-understanding in the ontological order: it is because we tacitly interpret nature as the locus of the realisation of pure logic, and conceive logic on the model of the formal systems with which we are by now familiar, that we can presume ourselves to have critically understood the natural world through the unreal schemas of pure formalism. This fore-understanding has developed historically. Whatever the intellectual motivation of its originators may have been, we are today faced with an already mature enough undertaking to demand an exact knowledge of its own presuppositions; but these presuppositions could not have come to be except by means of an experiment which, in principle, was pure risk. The prolonged testing of the proposed method has revealed its fertility and now obliges us to attempt to understand its foundation and to discover its *a priori* justification.

5. THE HUMAN SCIENCES

Development in the human sciences has been influenced in part by development in the natural sciences. Despite some prejudices and too precipitous considerations on the role of conscience or freedom it has become evident that the realm of human action does not escape the well-tried methods of the natural sciences. This became obvious in the first place in the areas where quantification or at least statistical manipulation was possible. But as was noted earlier the applicability of the empirico-formal method is in no sense essentially bound to quantification understood as expressible in numerical form. The fertility of algebraic methods in the human as well as in the physical domain shows that it is possible to disclose by formal means purely relational aspects of reality. 'Structuralist' approaches are a good example of this development for in the measure that these approaches become rigorous they lead to the adoption of algebraic language and so open the way to an explanation of the formal type.

The empirico-formal method showed its power first of all in those domains which, by reason of their abstraction, lent themselves easily enough to formalisation. So it was with political economy which became mathematical by way of pure economics. But here one is in a domain where abstractive idealisation is, as it were, visibly preformed in the reality. To the extent that economic relationships are established that have to do with goods and services which are easily isolated and defined in themselves independently of any actors, it is a relatively simple matter to detach these relations from the existential situations in which they emerge, to consider them in their pure form and to develop an abstract theory about them. However, there are domains in which the process of abstractive idealisation, which is the condition of formalisation, is less visible. Such is the case with cultural anthropology. It may be thought that the only adequate way to understand a culture is to grasp it as a totality, to re-live it, to enter into it, to so put it on as to integrate it in its proper lived cultural field. The language proper to cultural anthropology would then be a sort of poetic language which, through symbols, would enable the readers to share in the lived experience of the anthropologist. In other words, there would be no scientific anthropology in the strict sense. The structuralist school, however, has shown that it is possible to impose on cultural realities a model revelatory of systems of relations and to subject these systems to a formal analysis. Structuralism has shown that this kind of analysis can even be applied to elements which at first sight seem furthest removed from formalism, such as myths and symbolic systems in general.

Concomitant with this formalising tendency, there has been developed within the human sciences another and apparently totally different orientation: hermeneutics. The historical disciplines already posed the problem of interpretation. When there is question of understanding a past action or the meaning of a text, the only appropriate method seems to be a rehearsal of the development of the constituting intentionality which was the source of the action or of the text. What enables us to understand a historical actor is his intentions—that is, the relation between his actions and their motivations and goals. Clearly, the meaning of a historical action is not plumbed when its subjective meaning is known; there is the further question of the place of this action in the general flow of events. The action is defined not only by its 'for-itself', but likewise by its 'for-others'. Still the subjective meaning of an action is one of the dimensions of its meaning and the disclosing of this meaning involves an elucidation of the subjective life of the actor. Put another way, it consists in replacing the action in the concrete development of a person—that is, in the life of his projects and finally, little by little, in the totality of his existence. Similarly, the understanding of a text brings one back to the signifying intention of the author. To be sure, we have no direct access to the projects of the historical actor or to the intentions of a writer. Indeed, this is precisely why interpretation is needed. For what we have access to is only a result, a frozen expression. We cannot understand these data for what they are—manifestations of a human project—unless we consider them as manifestations of an expressive act, unless we succeed in moving from their given meaning to their giving meaning, from their pure phenomenality to the intentional life which generated them.

The search for meanings thus understood consists in inventing hypotheses to cover the generating intentions, and on their bases trying to reconstitute the visible aspects of the action. And in this sense there is no difference between the method of interpretation and the empirico-formal method; in both cases one has recourse to hypothesis (that is to theory), to deductive explanation and to the empirical verification of the hypotheses. But this analogy seems fairly external. For what is important is the nature of the hypotheses invented. Now in the case of the empirico-formal sciences hypotheses are propositions of a formal system and take their meaning only from their situation within the framework of the system. Their meaning is specified by the rules (of construction and derivation) of the system—that is, by the operative manipulations in which they appear or to which they give rise. In the hermeneutic sciences, hypotheses regard intentionalities.

Not is seems difficult to conceive intentionality on the model of formal entities. And it is hard to see how to reduce a description of intentionality to an operative schema. In the operation purely abstract terms are related according to rule; the terms intervene in the process only in their function as terms. This establishment of interrelations between terms is external to the terms which, accordingly, do not encroach on each other. Intentionality is a relation of transcendence; it is consciousness going outside itself, or more exactly it is consciousness in so far as it is continually going beyond, openness, movement beyond itself, call, demand, desire. In its going beyond itself whether in knowledge when it loses itself in the object, or in willing when it links itself with the other, or whatsoever, consciousness continues to remain with itself. In going beyond itself we might say that it envisages the world as an infinite system of its own possibilities, or that it envisages itself as the truth of all its partial experiences and of the world to which it has access. In intentionality consciousness and world belong reciprocally together; the terms thus encroach upon each other.

If intentionality is not operation, then it cannot be understood as operation—that is, by abstract effectuation. It is not possible, in the last analysis, to re-effect the intentional movements of a consciousness, to re-live its dream, its desire or its remorse. None the less, intentionality is accessible to us in the reflexive act which allows us to retrieve and explicate what is tacitly exercised in consciousness. Critical reflexion is obviously something quite different from the psychological event of becoming aware of something. It is rather a systematic effort at analysis, which attempts to follow the real links of conditioning underneath conscious

10

activities to enable it to disclose the universal forms of egological life.

The recent development of the human sciences has demonstrated that the life of meanings is more complex than it seemed when the model was rational action in which in principle there is perfect correspondence between the actor's lived meaning and the meaning brought to light in interpretation. The problem of interpretation appears very different when one is dealing with irrational actions and behaviour. The first reaction is to think of irrationality as a sort of inexplicable residue, or as an intrusion into the domain of action of disturbing factors of purely physical or biological origin. On this view the irrational is outside the domain of meaning. But a resolute insistence on understanding uncovered a hidden rationality in irrational behaviour which, no less than rational behaviour, belonged to consciousness. At a stroke, the field of understanding was broadened: to grasp the meaning of an action it was no longer sufficient to relate it to the explicit intentions of the actor, nor even to his implicit projects in so far as these could be derived from his conscious projects. And even in cases where such interpretation was possible, still it was necessary to disclose a hidden life of meaning which did not reveal itself within the field of explicit consciousness except in enigmatic images which at times were no better than camouflage.

This hidden life of meaning is, in one way, external to consciousness. It seems to come from elsewhere. Still it appears as a setting up of meanings, as a positing of signifiers whose whole function is to lead to a lived action with which they do not coincide, as a play of hidden intentionalities. Therefore, these cannot be understood save by means of those concepts which have already served to elucidate the life of consciousness proper. The constitution of meaning outside consciousness seems to reduplicate consciousness within itself and sets up beneath the level of consciousness a signifying activity which does not seem to be the activity of a subject.

In the light of these remarks two strategies are possible. On the one hand, taking it that the genesis of non-apparent meanings occurs outside consciousness, one can set oneself to understand this genesis on the model of a formal mechanism. And thus one adopts the empirico-formal method. But then it is only by an abuse of language that one speaks of signification, intentionality and, more generally, of meaning. It remains to be explained, of course, how the products of these formalisable operations can be inserted into the intentional life, and how they can appear homologous to the products of that intentional life. But at all events the programme is clear: the operations apparently constitutive of hidden instances of egological life are to be reduced to formally comprehensible operations of the same type as those employed successfully in the account of physical phenomena.

On the other hand, taking account of the fact that the hidden meanings, while not directly apparent, still are true relations of signification, one can set oneself to understand this hidden signifying activity on the basis of what reflexion teaches about visible signifying acts. This implies, naturally, that the traditional conception of consciousness be widened as well as the concepts that were considered sufficient to account for the life of consciousness. In particular, the concept of intentionality has to be reformulated. But the explanation will remain a hermeneutic, that is a disclosure of meanings and so the linking of meaningful products with constituting intentionalities whether anonymous or personal, whether belonging to chtonian or egological consciousness, which are at the source of these products and to which the products point.

It must be stressed that interpretative understanding, as operative understanding, aims in its own fashion at system, although it is not the system of all the possible forms of operative construction. It is rather the system of all intentionalities. It stems from the nature of the intentional relation that recourse to intentionality reveals the demand for system. Whatever its particular form, intentionality is reference. The disclosure of the functioning intentionalities which underlie the visible products of human life must then be a description of the complete network of these references by following their indications until one reaches the ultimate referential which can only be the total system of all references, that is the life of signification itself. Depending on the way in which one follows the movement of intentionality this ultimate horizon will appear either as the complete system of all the possible terms in principle accessible to the subject —that is, as world, or as the foundational constituting activity which particular intentionalities specify. These are merely two different ways of undertaking the same reading, for in both cases what is aimed at is the universal life of meaning as source of all meaningful constructions.

Just as pure thought, as thought of the operation, is in the end thought of itself, since it is not thought of the operation except in so far as it is itself operation, so hermeneutical reflexion appears in the last analysis, inasmuch as it is the manifestation of meanings, as grasp of meaning by itself, for in it meanings appear in their signifying function and this function does not point to any privileged object or any closed domain, but to a fundamental movement of disclosure, which is existence itself, which is nothing other than the pure emergence of meaning, the coming to light of signification. As operation is understanding of itself as operation, so signification is signification of itself as activity. But while operative thought is only pseudo-reflexion since it is always outside itself and that not so much in its product as in the self-carrying movement of operations—that is, in the auto-production of the absolute formal field, the progressive unveiling of signifying life as the ultimate term of reference of all significations is truly reflexion, because in it the signifying life is interiorised, is re-established on the basis of its products and re-makes, so to speak, in the second moment of critical thought, the original act of production by which it establishes itself as signifying life.

6. PHILOSOPHY

The determination of the ultimate destiny of hermeneutics as interiorisation of signifying life leads us to an area of knowing on the borders of science and philosophy, and, in reality, introduces us to the proper domain of philosophy. Up to now, we have considered hermeneutics only as method of the human sciences. The aim of philosophy goes beyond this. It is a generalised hermeneutic and reflexion. As we have seen, formal science tends towards system, but the absolutely formal field, which represents the empty anticipation of a total system, is not the absolute field as such. It is rather a kind of *a priori* with respect to the 'physis', and no doubt represents only a particular region of the *a priori*, namely the region which we have characterised as the domain of operations. Similarly interpretation tends towards the totality of signifying life. But the signifying life, as an anthropology might envisage it, is not absolute life. Philosophy begins as soon as thought becomes capable of revealing the dimension of universal life as absolute.

This disclosure no doubt demands a preliminary reductive step which, guided by the programmatic notion of a truly ultimate foundation for the system of givens (in evidence), of constructions (in operation) and of signification (in the life of meaning), is led to eliminate progressively the foundational attempts that are locked in particularity. Then, piecemeal, there arises the perspective of a knowledge that is not particular or specialised—not of forms, or nature, or action—but a universal knowledge, that is a knowledge of the totality, not in the sense of a system containing all knowledge, but in the sense of an understanding of universal foundations. The first moment of the enquiry introduces the theme of universal life. It is a moment at once regressive and progressive, which leads both towards a return to the absolutely initial foundational level, and towards an enlargement of horizons ending in the final horizon of universal development.

The truly characteristic task of philosophy begins with

the elucidation of the nature of universal life. How is one
to think totality as totality, foundation as foundation, or
quite simply, life as such, except by making the attempt to
conceive it on the model afforded by the analysis of our own
action? Just as the elucidation of this action must lead us
progressively towards the discovery of a constituting activity,
wholly immanent in the particular actions which it produces
yet at the same time infinitely removed from them in the
inexhaustibility of its infinite power, so the understanding of
the universal life demands that we grasp it at its source, in
the central point whence it unfolds, in an original action of
which the constituting activity of the egological life can be
only a distant 'analogon'. In different terms, the philosophic
effort must take the form of a theory of constitution. The
universal life, as absolute genesis of all forms and of all
significations, is in itself constituting act. To understand the
universal life is to place oneself within this constituting
activity in such a manner as to be present in its unfolding,
in such a manner as to coincide with its absolute constituting
activity.

Two fundamental questions arise: by what method can
one manage to coincide with the absolutely originating
constituting activity, and on what model can it be represented? To these questions the great philosophic systems
offer different answers. Some suggest a special mode of
knowing such as intuition, others rely on regressive analysis
which treads its way from condition to condition until the
supreme condition is reached, yet others call on reflexion.
In each case the choice of method determines the choice of
model. If one relies on intuition, the model will be a simple
act of retrieval and unfolding. If one chooses regressive
analysis, the model will be that of the phenomenal concatenation which proceeds by the disclosure of determining
conditions. As for reflexion, its model will be the act of
reflexion itself. To fill out these brief remarks would call for
a history of the great systems but we must be content to
recall that the type of understanding proper to the mode of

philosophic intelligibility is that of a thought which intends to retrieve and coincide with an absolute origin.

The proper unfolding of such a thought will be a repetition, in the representation, of the unfolding of the origin—it is thus that it becomes a thinking of constitution. Like all forms of critical thought, philosophical thought aims at the real, as it is given, and that through system. Its proper manner of retrieving the real is to understand it in its genesis. Nor is this genesis arbitrary. Rather it is the setting up of order of which it is itself the principle. In so far as it is pure unfolding, absolute genesis must be the setting in motion of a law which coincides with its nature. To the extent that thought becomes able to rejoin this absolute genesis, it becomes capable of grasping this law and thence understanding the unfolding of the world not as a mere fact but as the manifestation of a hidden law, as the fruit of a will for order; accordingly, as an organised whole the parts of which are linked together according to a network of necessary relations. The disclosure of the law of the formation of the whole, grasped on the level of its origin, in its constituting and self-constituting functioning, must clearly be in the form of a system. Whether the system itself takes the form of an explication of the content of absolute substance, or of a total reflexion in which the life of absolute spirit is revealed, or of a description of the becoming in which the absolute makes itself, or of a description of the hierarchy of the degrees of being according to the analogy schema, or some other form, we always discover the concern for connexion, founded here in the unificatory demand which is that of the absolute source itself.

So knowledge diversifies, intelligibilities multiply, the logos fragments. No doubt its diverse historical appearances are called to find their unity, in the time of fulfilment, in the form of a communal celebration of truth, but we have no means of representing that coincidence. We can only note differences and at best underscore analogies which establish a secret communication between the various attempts at truth. There is no visible, explicit communication for us except in origins—that is, in the foundational intention of a universal critique, understood as the condition for the setting up of an adequate discourse—that is, of an exhaustive system of the word.

7. THE WORD OF FAITH

Whatever the nature of the system, whatever its fertility and its limitations, its word is always the impersonal word of the system, that of universal connexions. In the experience of faith the word has an essential role too. But it is not now the expression of a system which would give us another approximation to truth. Now the word is revelation—that is, the free disclosure of the plan of God for the world in which at the same time both the destiny of man and, in a sense, the being of God are concerned. To the revealing word the answer is the word of faith which is at once acceptance of what is spoken, hope in the promise, and willingness to give oneself to the work of God by wholly satisfying his will.

Whereas the discourse of learning is an attempt to recollect reality in a system and so finds its proper scope in the universality of abstraction, the words both of revelation and of faith relate to events, and are themselves constitutive of events: on the one hand, the events of the visible manifestation of God in Jesus Christ, and on the other hand, the event of conversion and confession of faith. Whereas the discourse of learning aims at a reduplication of reality and its inclusion within the context of a comprehensive word, the word of revelation and its correlative word of faith bring into being a new reality, the work of salvation, whose meaning is reducible neither to that of logos, nor to that of 'physis', nor to that of action, nor even to that of universal life. Certainly we are once more confronted with constituting activity. But this time there is no duplication of the action and its explanatory word, there is rather a strict simultaneity of constituting action and word, for here the word in its being spoken is the constituting act of the new creation which is the establishment of the kingdom of God.

It is true that revelation includes a relation to truth, in that it lends itself to an attempt to understand it, as does, for example, the reality of our experience. By affording us a glimpse of the mystery of God it gives us a vision of God—and correlatively, of man—which presents itself to understanding and gives rise to a knowledge of a particular kind, which attempts to explicitate what is given in faith. To the extent that revelation is not simply an appeal to will, but the manifestation of the mystery of God, it calls for a certain mode of understanding, a certain type of intelligibility, so that faith in fact includes learning. In order to situate this learning or knowledge correctly with respect to other modes, it must be related to its origin, it must be replaced in the living context of the revealing word. This word is neither a review nor a justification of experience, nor is it a purely historical discourse which would be relative only to a particular moment in a universal evolution, nor is it a purely dialogic discourse which would be meaningful only as a word addressed to a determinate person. In a sense no doubt it is all these things. But essentially it is proclamation and in the light of this all its other characteristics must be reinterpreted. It is the proclamation of the good news of salvation and this proclamation is not simply the communication of information, but rather the actual effecting of what it proclaims. It is, then, an operative word in an absolutely radical sense, in an absolutely originating way. Such an operation is obviously not to be confused with the formal operation, which is action in the void, the simulacrum of effectuation. We are here dealing with an absolutely concrete genesis, which is not merely the particularisation of a law of development contained in universal life, but a pure welling-up, an inaugurating break, in which all reality, including universal life, is judged and in which an absolutely original order, irreducible to any other, is founded.

Correlative to the word of revelation is the word of faith which is not an attempt to explicate the revealing word, nor simply historical discourse (although it is always historically situated), nor simply dialogic discourse (although it is responsive). Rather it too, as the affirmation of faith in the 'Credo' shows, is a proclamation. In this it resembles the revealing word: like it, in the act of speaking, it brings into being that which it speaks. As salvation coincides with its proclamation, so also does faith with its proclamation. The proclamation is not simply ratification, or simply cry of gratitude or of praise. It is an articulated discourse which brings into play precise terms and propositions with determinable meanings. In the discourse of proclamation the relation of faith to truth appears concretely. Any subsequent attempt to make the content of faith explicit must rely on what is spoken in the 'Credo'. The relation of faith to truth and the kind of intelligibility proper to it must be understood on the basis of the proclamation, as it essentially is, and not on the model of scientific or philosophic discourse.

Now the proclamation is not simply a sort of ratification of a set of propositions which are 'proposed for belief', as if it were a question of endowing with a coefficient of certainty, on the basis of certain adequately interpreted signs, propositions in themselves either doubtful or even incomprehensible. Nor is the proclamation the mere repetition of a sort of pre-established canon which, endowed with some magical power, would be efficacious by itself. Rather each time it occurs, it is a new act, it calls forth the world in a new way. The proclamation is a total existential step by means of which a man takes on himself anew, and as if for the first time, the work of salvation, unites his will to the saving will of God, and sets his course towards God by allowing himself to be guided by the indications which God has given and of which the words he proclaims constitute as it were the intelligible framework. There is, then, something to be understood. But what is to be understood is God himself inasmuch as he is the one who calls; what is to be understood is the revelation itself—that is, the act which opens a new field of understanding. It is true that within faith there is an understanding of faith, but this is clearly a secondary and derived aspect. The essential is that faith in its announcement open us to the mystery that it proclaims. Thus it takes on again its original proclamation. This understanding, which rests on willing acceptance and makes real that at which it aims, is clearly not purely and simply a work of intelligence. It might be called a work of the heart if this metaphor indicated that in this work an existence came to terms with itself, risked itself, decided what it was, as a whole, to be.

Being thus a word of the heart, the word of faith is always both comprehension and incomprehension of itself and of its object. This mixture of clarity and unclarity corresponds to what the term mystery would indicate. But here nothing is static. The understanding proper to faith is of infinite reach: whatever clarity is reached is never anything more than an indication of clarity not yet reached. So it is linked with hope: acceptance of revelation is identically hope in revelation, the entry into the disclosing event is identically the expectancy of the fullness of the disclosure. For the proclamation of faith is but a step in the ascent to God—an ascent which, as the mystics were never tired of repeating, is a progress in a clarifying darkness. In such a manner can the relation between faith and truth be illustrated. What is shown is a truth which is both an unveiling and a mere enunciation. What we can understand in the propositions that we proclaim is that which in them is promise of a future understanding. The relation between truth and faith is eschatological; at the same time entirely actual and entirely to come. In the 'Credo' there is truly realised what is announced, and at the same time, there is only the announcement of what is already realised. Because the intelligibility proper to faith is that of an eschatological truth we can understand how and why faith is at once the ratification of an already present truth and the effectuation of a truth to come; why, in faith, there is an effectuation of truth as well as the ceaseless verification of what is effected.

If the truth of which we speak in faith has this mysterious status, this is because it finds its ultimate foundation in the living Word who is revelation and who proclaims himself: 'I am the way, the truth, and the life'.

VII

Faith and Cosmology

I. INTRODUCTION

The topic suggested is 'myth and faith'. The present essay
will approach it by an examination of the relations between
faith and cosmological representations. For faith is not
merely an interior attitude; it involves an expression which
uses, among other kinds, cosmological representations. These
representations appear to be associated with myths or stories
of the mythic type. If one would understand the meaning of
what is aimed at in faith, then a proper interpretation of
these mythic representations is imperative. In one sense it
will be a matter of going beyond the myth in a language
that would be a pure carrier of the meaning, a language in
which the brilliance of the representation could not so
charm intelligence as to subvert the basic intentionality. On
the other hand, one must be careful to retain from the
representation anything supporting that intentionality,
anything that would help prevent it foundering in complete
indeterminacy, anything that would orient it in the direction
which enabled it to be, in the first place, an aim. Faith
needs, perhaps, some representation, since the existence of
a language both pure and meaningful is at least doubtful.
Pure mathematics is, perhaps, a pure language but, as
Russell profoundly remarked, in mathematics one doesn't
know what one is talking about. Does faith need cosmological representations? Can it tolerate them, possibly as
pedagogic devices? It will be a useful preliminary to these
questions to treat of the cosmological representations in their

own right and of the relations between them and myth. We may begin with an examination of the function of myth in cosmological thought.

2. MYTH AND COSMOLOGICAL THOUGHT

One can distinguish at least two functions of myth: a pedagogic and a foundational function. Myth is pedagogic in two ways: the pedagogy of going beyond and the pedagogy of constitutive thinking.

(*a*) *Myth as pedagogy of going beyond* (*transcendence*): Myth is primarily pedagogy of transcendence. Cosmologic thought is thought of the cosmos. However, the cosmos is not only the sum of things in the visible universe, the assembly of natural beings, the collection of things that have their principle of movement in themselves. Nor is the cosmos one immense thing enveloping all others like the image of the heavens as a sphere holding the fixed stars. The cosmos is what holds together all natural beings, commanding their appearance and disappearance, ruling their movements, associating each with the others in a universal interaction presided over by necessity. Now our thought spontaneously accords with the things in the midst of which we dwell and among which, at least from some viewpoints, we must number ourselves. For cosmic thought to be possible, thought must find the means to separate itself from things, to gaze beyond their appearance, to transcend the visible towards a non-visible that is irreducible to the visible and yet the condition of it. A speculative transcendence is required.

Such a movement of thought is possible only if the domain which stretches beyond the visible is in some sense already present. Thematic thought is never more than the acceptance of a more archaic thought, the actuation of an already present possibility. This domain must not be a pure beyond, a universe that has nothing to do with this one and is totally separated from it. It must be related to this world and its visibility since, as invisible, it is the possibility of this world.

How are we to move towards what is not given in the visibility of the seen if not by means of the instrument which can make the absent present and the inaccessible accessible, namely language? And how can language evoke this distant unseen kingdom except by relying on what we commonly see and finding there a model for the operation which must be achieved?

The cosmological myth is a myth of origin; cosmology is, in the first place, cosmogenesis. Myth accounts for the world by associating it with an original time when this world was made from some unformed and undifferentiated matter. The original time is not contemporary time and differs from it profoundly. The present time is passage, erosion, fall, disintegration, the menacing imminence of radical collapse, return to the undifferentiated state. The original time is active power, organising force always at work, working in the present, capable of indefinitely repeatable rejuvenation, capable of being called from the depths of its immemorial past, which has run its course, to save a present faced with dissolution. The present time is here but it is unstable and powerless. The original time is infinitely far away but is always active and undecayed. The origin is, then, at once near and far away. It is established in radical discontinuity with this world, but it can always be called on from within this world and its re-actualisation maintains the order of this world. The original acts are described on the model of contemporary acts which may be considered as images of those acts of which they are the models: generation, birth, making and production in general, whether this refers to the autonomous production of nature or the heteronomous productions of men.

Production is the establishment of a distancing relation between the terms implied—producer and produced—such that the producer has priority as the one who posits the relation. Since there is relationship, there is a connexion between the two terms but the nature of the connexion is that it establishes a distance, so great in fact that the product can lead its own life independent of the producer and can even survive him. On the basis of this model it is possible to represent the visible world in its totality as the product in a basic relation of production. In such a representation one can go beyond the visible world to a productive act in relation to which the visible world is at a distance—a distance that can be traversed but not overcome. So one transcends the actual to a beyond which is its condition. This beyond is thought as production. The model serves in two ways: it makes going beyond possible (in that it suggests a regress from generated to generator) and it makes an image of the beyond possible (in that it suggests the image of a process of becoming, of descent). However, the model does not play its role in the same way in both cases. In the first case there is a movement towards an originating term in so far as it is separated from the produced term, in so far as it is at a distance from it. The second case represents the originating activity itself as procession from an origin.

Visible production, then, supports a representative technique which enables thought to enter a field of non-visible reality to which the visible world as a whole is related as to an origin and which is, accordingly, a condition of the visible. The visible as a whole is the concern here, not as sum but as organisation, as a structural whole. So it is that in the mythic cosmogony there is a thematisation of what makes nature a unity—that is, a cosmos. So the domain in which cosmological thought has free rein is open. But this domain is not yet thought: it is only in its activity that the myth allows us access to it. For myth is a thought enveloped in operation: it signifies by accomplishing and to it may be applied Wittgenstein's theory of language. By playing the language game, by using the words according to the rules, as one moves the pieces around a chessboard, we make meaning appear. But the meaning cannot be thematised, for there is no second degree language which would tell what went on in the game. Yet when one has passed through the language, one has then grasped how it is with the world, one has risen to the viewpoint of the totality, one sees what makes the world, but one's vision cannot be uttered. The language game is the world game. To seize the world one has to get out of the world and to get out of the world one has to get out of language. And it is by language that we can get out of language. We understand the world in re-effecting it; our speech is this re-effecting but we cannot say what we have done when we have re-effected the world.

(b) *Myth as pedagogy of constitutive thought* (*thought about constitution*): In one sense, but only in one sense, speculative thought is an effort to say what is done in myth, to work out a reflexive, self-controlled language. It is reflexive thematisation, but only in one sense for it is also in the form of a re-effecting of the world that speculative thought attempts to understand the world. Mythic representation has done more than merely open the domain in which speculative thought can unfold; myth suggests a model for speculation. A pedagogy of transcendence, myth is also the imaginative matrix which allows cosmological thought to constitute itself as constitutive.

The cosmological myth is an account of cosmogenesis. It tells how the world was made, how the contemporary world that stands before our eyes developed from what went before, from the non-world, the formless. The myth retraces the generative steps that have led from this primordial past to the present. The schema of the representation is a successive unfolding in which there is a movement from homogenous unity to a qualitatively differentiated multiplicity, passing through all the intermediary stages which progressively ensure differentiation from the origin and establish the link between the primordial moment and the complex, moving and multiform structure in which our cosmos is produced.

We can examine the operation of constitutive thought by selecting some well-known examples to lead from pure myth to pure language through the impure language of philosophy. Our way will be from Hesiod to Plato to Kant to Einstein.

Hesiod's poem describes the organisation of the world in

11

the form of a genealogy of the gods. Broadly these are three successive generations marking three reigns. At first there is chaos, the non-differentiated, the obscure base on which the figures of this world will appear, faceless power symbolised by night but which escapes beyond representation as the mystery which penetrates all things and envelops all production, an origin before the origin, a measureless abyss which conceals the originating power manifest in every birth and to which everything returns; for being, in its emergence from birth, ceaselessly returns to its origin, ceaselessly achieves in its becoming the moment which brought it to light and thus takes its strength from its source. Then, abruptly and without explanation—for we are at the beginnings of explanation—the first couple emerge: the earth and sky. This is the prime opposition which breaks the undifferentiated unity and grounds the possibility of indefinitely repeated oppositions; it is the dyad, the principle of multiplicity. This dyad is not merely numerical but is also qualitative: on the one hand, light which is the ground of the possibility of the appearance of figures, principle of all delimitation, determination, the place in which particular forms are produced, milieu of their interaction and hence of their community; on the other hand, darkness, unyielding, opacity, which arrests the diffusion of light, yet which is a resting place, a base, which gives figures the flesh which they require if they are to be concretely visible and come down from the infinity of the empyrean heavens. The meeting of these two elements is the fundament of particular things; their production conditions further productions. Finally there is the birth of the Titans among whom is Chronos who devours his own children. Time is multiplicity in movement and so the principle of mobility in everything that moves itself. But it is devouring; as it calls forth new figures it prevents them from maintaining themselves in the stability of identity, in the coherence of unchangeable being, it takes them up in its own becoming and leads them to their dissolution, it touches them with the chill of death at the very moment that it gives them life. The figures of this generation correspond to a world still in travail, to a tumultuous clash of forces in which there remains something of the formless power of original chaos and yet in which a more stable organisation is prefigured. With the fall of the Titans the reign of Zeus begins. Zeus with his attendant gods represents order in a nature henceforth established according to rigorous laws, a nature on which it is possible to count and in which man finds a stable dwelling place under the protection of the tutelary goddesses who preside over stable communities, over lasting unions and over the works of peace which bring natural forces into the service of men. The reign of Zeus is not definitively established until after a fierce battle with the Titans who after their defeat are buried under the earth and whose impotent rage is manifested from time to time in natural cataclysms such as volcanic eruptions. The universe as cosmos, as organised structure, is thus supported by untamed archaic powers, while at the same time it results from a conflict between these powers and an ordering principle which is finally dominant. And in this conflict there reappears the primitive opposition between earth and sky, for Zeus is a celestial power while the Titans are bound to the earth. Though the world as cosmos is a victory for figuration, this figuration is not the production of pure forms, it must be thought of as the imposition of form on matter—and matter is resistance as well as support. The schema is, then, exactly that taken up by Plato: the descent of forms into receptive matter which is both the necessary condition for the production of the visible as figure and an alien power which opposes its own law—a law of obscure and blind necessity—to the sovereign illumination of the intelligible.

Let us consider the Platonic cosmology in more detail. Its guiding idea is that of an organising process. Its model is the artist who, to make his work, uses pre-existing material and follows the indications of an image produced by his creative thought. The central figure in which the thought of the cosmos is expressed is the figure of the demiurge. To grasp its meaning we must relate it to the general principle of explanation in Plato's thought. Finite, multiple and changing things must be explained by simple essences: on one side, the model; on the other, the receptacle. The finite thing is the result of a union of these two essences. The demiurge represents their being brought together, the appropriation of one by the other, the descent of forms into the receiving matter, the meeting as such. The criterion for this action is the principle of the better, which when brought into play resembles a calculation of an *extremum*: it is a matter of finding the conditions which allow a quantity to receive either the greatest or least possible value when certain constraints are taken into account. Now the quest for an *extremum* is mathematisable; it is bringing an intelligible into play. Accordingly the principle of the better is a demand for what is most intelligible. The task of the demiurge will be to conform as perfectly as possible to the model that is intelligible in the pure state.

The cosmos as such is intermediary between the model and finite things. The analogy of the living thing is used to describe it; the cosmos has soul and body. The soul of the cosmos is older than its body in that it is its condition of possibility. It is the encircling heaven, unique, solitary, self-sufficient, knowing and loving itself, holding all things within its boundaries and thus relating all things among themselves. It is present everywhere, extended throughout the whole cosmos. It is, then, intermediary reality, mediation between the pure figures of the model and the body of the world. It is itself in relation, a close mingling of two essences: the indivisible, unvarying substance: the same, and the divisible substance which is in the body: the other. It is the soul that is animating principle of life and movement; 'it is extended in every direction, from the centre to the extreme heavens, encircling it from without'.

The soul of the world is numerical; both from a cardinal and an ordinal viewpoint. It is constituted of a succession of numerically ordered terms which define a series of intervals corresponding to a determinate generative law. Now a number series is its own becoming, it is number in movement. It is the ordinal essence of the soul which makes it the movement of the heavens. A series is not set in motion from the outside—its generative law is immanent and it is itself the principle of its unfolding; so the soul is self-moving, it is movement which moves itself and in this sense it is intellect. It is also time,'this eternal image which moves according to numerical law' and as such it is an 'image both eternal and changing' of 'eternity unmoved and one'. Time is the relation of the identical to itself in a distance always over-come and always renewed. In this sense it is an unceasing unsuccessful effort to regain the simplicity without distance where the identical is always with itself.

It is, then, as number that the soul is intermediary. Number is essentially between pure intelligibility and the visible. It is not pure idea since it is indefinitely multipliable and so does not possess the absolute simplicity of the idea. Neither is it a sensible thing since it is the organising principle of the sensible and can be thought apart from the realities it enumerates. Now what are the conditions of the possibility of number and number organised in a series? First, a multiplicity and then an ordinal principle acting on the terms of the multiplicity. Multiplicity is given in the original rupture of unity. It is the fruit of the action of the other on the same. It represents the original act in which the same is separated from itself and produces itself outside itself as otherness. Ordering is the repetition of the original rupture of unity, it is the progressive generation in which otherness appears as the series of unsuccessful attempts to stabilise unity, as setting the simple in motion as pure succession. Number is pure movement, it is time; being pure positing of movement, being movement without figure, it founds all concrete figured movements.

So is complete the table of all the elements that compose the soul of the world: the same and the other, time, number, movement. These elements belong mutually to each other and so form a foundational unity. The same and the other constitute the original duality, the principle of pure multiplicity. Time mediates the fundamental otherness in the form of becoming. It posits itself as ordered but still symmetric multiplicity. (The figure of time is the circular movement of the heavens which continually repeats itself, and where every point periodically returns to its original position.) Time posits itself as such by the power of number, ordered self-generating multiplicity, series which posits itself in the regular development of its terms. In so far as it is ordered by number, time is pure movement, the principle of all concrete movements. Time, then, is the essence of mobility, entering into everything and carrying everything with it in its original movement. Every concrete movement is made possible by the fundamental movement which is pure succession: this is the movement of the soul, the movement of the heavens, time. Time grounds movement by the intermediary of number just as number is the movement of the world as time. We have, accordingly, a foundational sequence in which is thematised the problem of multiplicity as movement, and in which the possibility of movement in general and of all concrete movements in particular finds its *a priori* foundation.

The cosmos comes into being when the soul enters the body of the world. The body is composed of the four elements which are themselves reducible to various combinations formed of two basic triangles. The elements pre-exist the action of the demiurge, but before the formation of the world they are 'without reason or measure', they 'were in that state natural to things in the absence of the god'. From him they received their forms 'by the action of ideas and numbers'. These forms are the cube, the tetrahedron, the octohedron, and the icosahedron corresponding respectively to earth, fire, air and water. These forms may be generated from two basic geometric entities, namely two types of right-angled triangle. The first type is the right-angled

isosceles triangle, in which the two sides forming the right
angle are equal. All triangles of this kind are similar. We
are dealing here with the simplest form and for this reason
the cube which can be formed with twenty-four of these
triangles corresponds to the element which is both the most
solid and the most difficult to move, namely earth. The
second type is the right-angled scalene triangle in which the
sides of the right angle are not equal. This type of triangle
may be realised in infinitely many ways. Among these, one
is remarkable: that in which the smaller of the two sides is
equal to half the hypotenuse. From six of these triangles can
be constructed an equilateral triangle and from equilateral
triangles so constructed can be generated polyhedra of four,
eight and twenty faces.

However, ideas and numbers are not sufficient to establish
the elements; there is still required the place of their production. This place appears as a support, a sort of prime
matter, as the condition of the possibility of transmutations
and as the condition of the possibility of the multipliability
of figures. Change and multiplicity suppose an otherness
which will not be simply logical otherness as given in pure
multiplicity. There is demanded a physical otherness, a
principle of dispersion and extraneousness. We can see here
the role of the *chôra* which is at once space and support, a
system of places and the universal place of the figures.

None the less it is in the model that the world as we know
it, as it stands before us, finds its explanation. The demiurge
merely represents in the image of a sublime artisan the
action of the model. And the model, the domain of intelligibility is itself organised; it constitutes a unified system
under the aegis of a single principle, a primary idea above
every other idea: the *agathon*. The perfection of the *agathon*
is diffused throughout the complex and hierarchic set of
ideas. But this diffusion is purely logical, it forms an
intelligible spectrum, a system of pure links; the universe of
ideas as unified by the power of the *agathon* is the framework
of the world. This internal diffusion which indwells the

world of ideas and makes the model into a living thing is reproduced in the production of the world.

If there is internal movement by which the one is diffracted into the pure multiplicity of the idea, there is external movement by which the idea itself diffracts into the visible multiplicity of the concrete world, and this movement, represented by the action of the demiurge, repeats the first. To become visible, however, the intelligible has need of a place. To manifest itself, to enter the realm of appearing, the pure form must be received, imprinted, incarnated. It cannot take on its visible body unless it is immersed in a milieu that can arrest its diffusion and so force it to produce itself in the bounded space of a sensible form. The pure figure cannot enter into the flux of change until it pits itself against the pure primordial flow in which everything can become everything else. The world as it is, an immense living thing shot through by intellect and led inexorably in unceasing becoming, is conditioned: on the one hand, there is required an intelligible framework, the model, and on the other hand a receptive principle, the *chôra*. However the model cannot be related to the *chôra* except through an intermediary. It is the function of the world soul as time to ensure the mediation between these two essences, thus allowing sensible things to be produced in the process of the idea becoming finite and so projecting the invisible in the corruptible and at the same time placing the corruptible in the life of the eternal.

The construction found in the *Critique of Pure Reason* is close to that of the *Timaeus*. Needless to say the context is different for in the *Critique* the problem is the basis of the possibility of knowledge, that is a theory of the *a priori*. Still, the knowledge in question is knowledge of nature. The critical effort, at least in its positive aspect, refers primarily to the possibility of physics. And the theory of physical knowledge must also be a philosophic theory of nature. For Kant the theory of nature is the study of the *a priori* foundations of theoretical physics. The transcendental aesthetic and the transcendental analytic provide the purely *a priori* elements of knowledge of nature. As is clear from the *Metaphysical Principles of the Science of Nature*, the philosophy of nature which constitutes the *a priori* part of the science of nature and provides the *a priori* foundations for the principles of Newtonian mechanics consists in applying the principles of the critique to an elementary empirical datum—motion— showing how the physical object is constituted and revealing its intelligible structure.

The principles of Newtonian mechanics result from the application of the principles of pure understanding to this content. The axioms of the intuition yield the principle of (classical) relativity. The anticipations of perception yield the principles of the theory of matter as a system of attracting and repelling forces and so ground a theory of gravity. The analogies of experience yield the fundamental axioms of rational mechanics. The principle of permanence yields the principle of conservation of momentum which contains the principle of inertia. The principle of production provides the fundamental principle of dynamics (the proportionality of force with respect to acceleration) and the principle of community provides the principle of the equality of action and reaction. Finally the postulates of empirical thought in general ground the distinction between relative and absolute motion.

Thus the key to the knowledge of nature is found in the *Critique*. The philosophy of physics is a philosophy of nature. Passage from one to the other is grounded in the terms of the *Critique* itself. It is justified and understood in the light of the basic principle of the *Critique*, namely that the con- ditions of the possibility of experience are the conditions of the possibility of the objects of experience. We are thus faced with a cosmology in the critical sense, namely a science of the principles of the possibility of the objects of physics, or a science of the principles of the possibility of a system of objects as cosmos. Even the idea of cosmos as

totality is an idea of reason to which there is no corresponding
intuition. Accordingly this idea gives rise to the cosmological
antinomies. But precisely as an idea of reason it provides a
guideline for constructing a general science of phenomena.
The issue here is the internal organisation of the cosmos seen
in the perspective of an enquiry into the conditions of
possibility of phenomena, that is the cosmos as phenomenon
(not as noumenon).

No object is available to us except through the meeting of
form and content; the object presupposes a given and a
unification. But the occurrence of a given presupposes a
correlative receptivity. Our sensibility submits to the given
in that it is the capacity to receive representations dependent
on the way objects affect us. However, a unification of the
diversity presented in the content is still required and it is
here that one may locate the *a priori* as foundational domain.
The foundational action of this domain is understood as an
act of unification which is nevertheless also an act of diversi-
fication. It may be thought of as subsumption: the operation
in which the diverse is progressively unified. The initiative
necessarily belongs to a unifying principle which can operate
only by diffusing its unity to the boundaries of the multiplicity which it must synthesise. This diffusion develops by
a series of steps: there is the purely logical level of the judgement, there is space which is the level of diversity closest to
sensible multiplicity and there is the intermediary level of
time which is thought according to the theory of the
schematism. The mediation of time makes motion intelligible
and so grounds the possibility of physics as rational
mechanics.

Judgement engenders a synthesising activity and so a
principle of unity which covers the whole domain of logic
and through it all the levels of the constitution of the object.
This principle is the activity which founds the object by
the intermediary of mediations through which it is diffracted.
This is the originating synthetic unity of apperception, the
foundation of all unity, the central synthesising activity, the

identity of the 'I think' with itself throughout a multiplicity of representations, the 'transcendental principle of the unity of knowledge in the synthesis of the diversity of our intuitions'. The 'I think', to the extent that it is synthesised with itself and remains with itself in every synthesis that it achieves, is the foundation of the *a priori* and grounds its foundational power. Transcendental apperception works through the categories of understanding. The act by which the diversity of given representations is subsumed in the unity of consciousness is the judgement. In judgement the synthesis joins the given, in judgement unity descends to multiplicity. The modes in which this descent occurs are the modes in which the judgemental synthesis can function, 'the logical functions of judgement'. The categories 'are nothing else than these same functions of the judgement in so far as the diversity of a given intuition is determined in relation to them'.

Understanding is related to intuition through the schematism. The necessity of the schematism results from the nature of the terms in question: the concepts of the understanding are totally heterogeneous with respect to empirical intuitions. And their function is to apply to these intuitions and they have neither meaning nor value beyond this reference. The possibility of application is grounded in a third term which will be homogeneous with respect to both category and intuition. This third term appears as a pure intermediary representation, *a priori*, both intelligible and sensible. The schematism provides these representations. The schematism is essentially the mediation of time. Time, as the form of pure succession, is the diverse subjected to rule and so to synthesis; it is pure vision of succession and rule only to the extent that in it the principle of synthesis appears in an image of connexion. Time is pure intuition. It is neither concept nor phenomenon but it is homogeneous with both concept and phenomenon—homogeneous with concept to the extent that it includes in itself the exercise of rule *a priori*; and homogeneous with phenomenon

in that it 'is included in every empirical representation of
the diverse'. 'Application of the category of phenomena is
possible through the transcendental determination of time
and this determination as the schema of the concepts of
understanding serves to subsume phenomena under the
category.' The schema—that is, the *a priori* representations
mediating the relation of category to empirical intuition—
are then the different ways in which time can be affected
by the categories, or conversely the different ways in which
the categories can be diffracted in time. Quantity gives time
as series, quality gives time in its content, relation gives
time as order and finally modality gives time as a whole
and 'in relation to all possible objects'. With time number
is rediscovered; for number is time as affected by quantity.
'The pure schema of quantity, considered as a concept of
the understanding, is number which is the representation
embracing the successive addition of unity to the homogeneous. So number is the unity of the synthesis operated in
the diversity of a homogeneous intuition in general, by the
very fact that I produce time itself in the apprehension of
the intuition.'

Finally with the schema we come to the final figure of
unification. Already close to the pure multiplicity of the
diverse, it is, in fact, space. The kind of change proper to
space is not the kind proper to quantity. Quantity is category,
pure synthesis. Space is intuition. It is *a priori* since it serves
as foundation for exterior phenomena which cannot be
perceived outside space. Further the principles of the science
of space, geometry, possess apodictic certainty. It is, however, intuition not concept, for geometrical propositions are
synthetic *a priori* not analytic and intuition is required for
the synthesis. Besides, only a single space can be represented
and when the parts are to be distinguished these are not
subsumed under space as elements but are thought in it.

Kant contemplated nature philosophically through the
representations of Newtonian mechanics. Constitutive
thought in modern physics takes the form of general rela-

tivity. The idea of the Einsteinian theory of general relativity
was to give an entirely geometric representation of gravity.
In classical physics there are three terms: space (conceived
as container and described in euclidean terms), particles
(occupying space and characterised by their kinematic
properties and by a purely intrinsic determination and
measure of their inertia, mass) and forces (representing the
the interactions between particles). In relativity physics we
retain only space and particles. But space is no longer merely
a container; it includes force. Thus equipped with physical
properties it becomes a field. So it is no longer possible to
talk of homogeneous space, exterior to the particles, independent of matter, without proper content. We are, rather,
faced with a space endowed with differentiated content with
variable regional properties. The properties of the space
explain the behaviour of the particles which move within it.
The geometrisation of physics is at the same time a physical-
isation of geometry.

Relativity physics substitutes riemannian for euclidean
space. From the geometric viewpoint the non-null curvature
of riemannian space distinguishes it from euclidean space
(it is in terms of curvature that one can account for the
difference between a section of a spheric and a plane
surface). From the physical viewpoint, the curvature corresponds to the presence of gravity. The gravitational field is
described by ten structural conditions imposed on the
curvature of a four-dimensional riemannian manifold. On
this basis the principle of inertia can be generalised. In
classical mechanics, the principle of inertia asserts that a
body left to itself (that is free of all external force) conserves
its state of motion indefinitely—that is, it moves in a straight
line at a constant velocity. In relativity mechanics the
principle of inertia asserts that in empty space (in the
absence of matter) a body describes a geodesic of riemannian
space—that is, moves from one point in this space to another
along the shortest path between the two points. But in
riemannian space the shortest path between two points is

not necessarily a straight line. In fact it is a straight line only when the intensity of the gravitational field in the region is zero.

Relativity gravitational theory suggests two lines for theoretical research: first, the extension of relativity theory into electro-magnetism; secondly, the suppression of the field-particle duality. The first problem calls for the integration of the set of electro-magnetic phenomena into the framework of general relativity. But this cannot be done by adding to riemannian space new conditions over and above those already imposed on it by the theory of gravity. Therefore the framework of the existing theory must be enlarged, and this can be done in either of two ways. Either one retains riemannian space but adds new dimensions, or one has recourse to non-riemannian theories. The first possibility leads to theories that are of necessity somewhat artificial given that real space has four dimensions. The second approach, then, seems the more interesting. A geometric entity of more general character is needed. Use will be made of a manifold with general affine connexion. A manifold of this kind presents three characteristic properties relevant for theory: torsion, rotational curvature, and homothetic or segmentary curvature. Torsion may be explained thus:

When the torsion is non-zero, in euclidean space tangent to the manifold (i.e. touching the manifold at a certain point), the correspondent of an infinitely small closed contour within the manifold is itself non-closed.

Rotational curvature corresponds to the ordinary notion of curvature: it expresses the difference with respect to the euclidean character (for example in relation to the planar character in the case of a two-dimensional space). Finally, segmentary curvature may be explained as follows:

When the curvature is non-zero the standard of length is not constant under transformation. (In other terms: the length of a vector displaced parallel to itself along an infinitely small closed contour on the manifold does not remain constant.)

A euclidean manifold is one without torsion or curvature. A riemannian manifold is one without torsion or homothetic curvature but possessing rotational curvature. A generic manifold possesses both torsion and the two kinds of curvature. And it is precisely this type of general manifold that was used by Einstein in his final theory.

The second problem is the duality of particle and field in the relativity gravitational theory. This duality can be an irritant to the kind of thought that is taken up with unity. The sources of the field should be reducible to the field itself. In Einstein's later work the particles are integrated into the structure of the field. Matter is assimilated to those regions of space where the intensity of the field is of very high value, that is to singularities of the field which are spatially displaced in the course of time and whose displacement corresponds to the movement of bodies as we can observe them. Along these lines, matter is entirely reducible to field which becomes the unique physical reality. In his later speculations Einstein attempted to extract matter from the purely geometric properties of the generalised field. However, the success of the programme depends on the expression being able to contain the contribution of the electro-magnetic field and so the two problems merge in the general idea of a physics of pure field, that is a total geometrisation of physics.

Of course a complete general field theory would have to include quantum mechanics and here there are considerable if not insurmountable difficulties. But the way opened by general relativity to a generalised field physics is without any doubt the most speculative and profound possibility of modern physics. What is the general idea of the step which characterises relativity theory as field theory? It consists of giving to a manifold (that is to a punctual multiplicity endowed with 'neighbourhood' properties), named space, conditions rich enough to obtain an adequate representation of phenomena, The starting point is a totally undifferentiated pure multiplicity, in mathematics called a set. The set is then provided with appropriate 'structures'. First a topological structure—that is, a notion of 'neighbourhood'—is defined on the set. (This notion permits one to give a meaning to the concept of continuity which plays a fundamental role as much in analysis as in geometry.) Then a metric is added, for a metric structure gives a meaning to the notion of distance. The metric allows the definition at each point of an infinitesimal length which in general varies from point to point. Finally the set is provided with an affine connexion. This consists in defining certain coefficients—the coefficients of affine connexion—which are themselves functions of coefficients occurring in the expression of the element of length (provided by the metric). The coefficients of affine connexion allow one to define at each point a correspondence between the euclidean space tangent at that point and the euclidean space tangent at a point infinitely close. In other words, it allows one to define in the euclidean space tangent at a point a representation of the manifold in the neighbourhood of that point. It may be said that the affine connexions describe the way in which neighbouring regions of the manifold are connected with each other. As indicated above, a manifold with affine connexion may have a torsion and two kinds of curvature. Three cases are possible: the torsion and the two curvatures may differ from zero, only the rotational curvature may differ from zero, the torsion and the two curvatures may be null. In the first case there is a general metric manifold of some kind; in the second case a riemannian manifold; in the third case a euclidean. It is clear that the process is a progressive enrichment of an undifferentiated multiplicity.

To the extent that one is successful in reducing the set of physical phenomena to the structure of space, one can account for whatever appears in terms of multiplicity. Starting from absolutely undifferentiated multiplicity one ends up with a multiplicity sufficiently organised to contain whatever is manifest in the visible world. Thus the visible world is generated entirely *a priori*, by passing from the

purely diverse, the purely abstract, to concrete diversity
under the forms of which nature is produced.

What is common to the theories we have examined?
Four common characteristics can be discerned:

(i) In each there is a theory of the cosmos which thinks
the cosmos is the form of a genesis. The theory describes the
generation of the world from an origin that is indeterminate,
undifferentiated and super-saturated in that it precontains
the entire process, encloses in advance in its unity all the
stages of the unfolding.

(ii) The development of the world towards its concrete
form from its origin is conceived as a process of diffusion
operating on successive levels or as a diffraction through a
series of surfaces. These levels or surfaces represent different
stages of conditioning. There is a set of interlocking conditions, each condition being both conditioned and conditioning, conditioned by the preceding condition and condition
of the subsequent condition. The condition is the condition
of the subsequent condition only to the extent that it is itself
conditioned by the preceding condition.

(iii) The ordered set of conditions forms the *a priori* of
visible things inasmuch as it allows them to form a real
cosmos. This *a priori*, being the foundation of things, necessarily precedes them and is not itself a thing. It is, in the
totality of its internal articulations, a conditioning factor, an
operative system of conditions.

(iv) Finally, each of these theories of constitution has
an operative aspect. Constitutive thought re-enacts the
production of visible things, it follows once again their
developmental way from their origin to their manifest being.
The intelligibility achieved in constitutive thought is thus
analogous to the intelligibility achieved in the calculus
when it allows us to reproduce in the abstraction of a
formalism the real operations that the formalism represents.
Thought of the cosmos reproduces in its own development
the original unfolding which posits the cosmos as cosmos
and in which the cosmos itself consists.

12

(c) *The foundational function of myth*: Having considered the pedagogic function of myth, we have now to envisage myth in its foundational function. The question is one of meaning. In this perspective myth appears as the original flowering of meaning. Cosmological thought is thought concerning the constitution of the world. How can this thought be meaningful? What is the meaning of constitution? How is it to be understood as such? Should we think of the emergence of this thought and so of the real constitution which it thinks, or of the terms of the process, or of its result? The result may be excluded for it is precisely its end product which constitutive thought has to found. It cannot take its meaning from that to which it gives meaning by its foundational function. Terms, too, should be excluded since no term is self-sufficient. The important thing, that which carries meaning, is the connexion between terms and their interrelations. Terms are connected by a connecting operation which is the proper task of constitution. So we are back with effectuation; to find the guideline of meaning we must grasp constitution in act, understand how it operates, seize it in its movement.

We may fruitfully consider the case of physics since it is the clearest and, in intention, perhaps the most radical instance. How does physical theory have a meaning? In physical theory there is internal coherence; a system of connexions, as system, carries a meaning which it evokes from within itself by its own movement. But this meaning is purely formal, which is to say that it relates to the mutual operation of signs on one another. As formal system the theory belongs to mathematics and is not yet thought of the world. For it to become physics it requires interpretation. What is the basis of the interpretation? According to a widely accepted view the interpretation of the theory is to be found in the experiments which the theory explains. Now it is certainly the case that theory has no physical meaning until it is related to possible experiments and so is susceptible of verification. But does this mean that the theory gets its meaning-content from the experiment? Could not the possibility of a relation with experiment presuppose a meaning-content which is there before the experiment is made? It is worth mentioning, too, that the experiments confirming relativity theory are few and of purely local import. What gives the theory its import and its true meaning are far more the organising ideas which gave rise to it than its experimental confirmation. Furthermore, the thought which inspired the theory goes far beyond anything that has been realised to date. The value of generalised field theory lies more in its programme and in the possibilities it reveals than in the constructions under which it appears at this time. And it has been accepted much more on account of its internal qualities than for its predictive capacity. The guide-line of thought concerning relativity is not to be found in the experiment, it is on the level of pure theory—and in the aesthetics rather than the pragmatics of thought. What captures the mind is its power of synthesis and unification, the breadth and radical character of the project, the expansive vision. A theory such as this cannot be considered as simply a predictive formalism. It presents itself as having explanatory value. It takes this value from itself, from its theoretic power, and not from some additive accruing to it from the experiment. In other words, its explanatory power and signifying force comes from an *a priori*.

Where, then, is this *a priori* to be found? Is it in the mind which posits the theoretic principles, as the Kantian interpretation of Newtonian mechanics suggests? This explanation hardly stands the test of the history of thought. Reliance on a purely formal subjective *a priori* seems quite inadequate to deal with the historicity of theoretical thought and of its internal fruitfulness which gives it consistence through successive apparent discontinuities. When one investigates the transition from classical to relativity mechanics it becomes clear that the advance was not due to a new initiative for synthesis in subjectivity, but to an internal exigence that physical theory as conceptual system contained within itself.

It is not consciousness which posits new forms. Nor is it the forms of consciousness that are objectified in new figures. It is the concept itself that raises itself to a more comprehensive level by relying on its own potentialities and by showing clearly, through the intermediary of fruitful contradictions, what it already obscurely indicated in its internal structure before reflexive consciousness was capable of remarking it. The theory has its own objectivity and dynamism which the mind only recognises and ratifies. It is in the theory or behind it, in what it effects or in what it inherits, that the secret of its meaning must be sought.

However, we cannot be content to concentrate exclusively on the internal connexions as they are implicitly posited in the system, for they provide no more than a formalism demanding interpretation. Now if the interpretation is not found in the experiment—that is, not found *a posteriori*, it must be *a priori*. An *a priori* interpretation seems to be the historicity of the theory—that is, its rootedness in other theories, its reference to an older, more original theoretic context. A theory of constitution cannot find its proper meaning, cannot present itself precisely as constitutive thought except in so far as it is situated in a context where this thought is already exercised and where the domain in which constitutive thought can occur is already revealed. It is, of course, possible to appeal from a formalised theory like physics to a theory closer to reflective language and consequently more capable of evoking in us, by a sort of resonance, a comprehension of the operations which reveal how the world is. Nevertheless, any theory of this sort, to the extent that it sets in motion foundational thought, to the extent that it opens the context of the *a priori*, presupposes the dimension of origin of the foundational.

Now, can we claim to be in such a dimension straight away? Do we not have to be led there? Have we not to learn to recognise nature and its laws from what we have learned from our sojourn among things? Myth, to the extent that it is that which effects the transition from the origin (in the empirical sense) to the originating, from visible origins to the *a priori* origin, introduces us to the originating domain. Can we understand the originating as dimension without relying on the origin as image, an image charged with transcending power? And can we be gripped by this transcending power without expressing it in the language of myth, the discourse in which the possibility of constitutive thought is first opened to us? So it seems it is with reference to the revealing power of myth that every theory of constitution takes its meaning—that is, its possibility of presenting itself as it is, namely, constitutive thought. Accordingly, as source, as first discourse, as source of meaning, myth is present within all theoretic thought as a kernel which theoretic thought necessarily resumes in itself, as a first operation which this thought necessarily takes up in its own development.

Myth is present as original effectuation providing in advance the schema of all effectuations. All constitutive thought is operative, a re-enactment of the production of the world. Myth is present to thought as that which begins and makes possible the characteristic operations of thought. Myth is present as foundation of meaning in that it is a pedagogy of effectuation, in which constitutive thought spreads its wings, and from which it gets the light that illumines its flight. Still the meaning that emerges in theoretic discourse is present only non-thematically in that discourse, for it is present to the theory only in a effectuation, namely in the theorising activity itself. So the re-effectuation of the world which is constitutive thought, is accompanied by a re-effectuation, in that thought, of the originating thought from which it springs, which remains its immanent examplar, and which has always opened it to its own possibility.

3. FAITH AND COSMOLOGICAL REPRESENTATIONS

We are now in a position to return to our problem of the

relation between faith and cosmological representations. The question is not simply that of the relation between faith and myth since myth is not to be identified with cosmological representation. Nevertheless, the question of the relation between faith and myth is relevant since myth is peculiarly related to cosmological representation in that it is at the source of thought of origins and in that this thought, in all its forms, belongs to the unfolding of a force which appears in its earliest form as myth. Two questions emerge: does faith necessarily explicate itself in a form which involves a cosmological representation? Is there a way leading from cosmological discourse to faith?

(*a*) *Discourse and word*: Investigation of the first question leads to a negative answer, and of the second to an answer that is affirmative but problematic. Every cosmological representation belongs to constitutive thought. Such thought is expressed in discourse and is itself discourse—that is, an ordered sequence of concepts linked together in some sense necessarily. Our discourse is of this kind only to the extent that, as constitutive discourse, it is the re-effectuation of the cosmologic operations. It recreates in itself the discourse of reality, the immanent logic of the cosmos which operates in it as the necessary concatenation of the moments of its foundation. The most perfect type of connexion is circular— that is, connexion which generates a system in which all the terms are mutually interconnected in the same manner and homogeneous with respect to their connecting force. Cosmological discourse is modelled on the circular figure, the accomplished systematic form. It is discourse of the eternal return, of repetition. In myth the beginning is replaced in the present inasmuch as the present is replaced in the original time. The beginning continually begins anew. In the attempts at speculative foundation we are dealing with a domain of the *a priori*, with a system of pure logic, whose originating force is constantly at work. We are in the presence of an origin which continually unfolds itself as foundation and is, thus, a perpetual reiteration of itself.

Is faith an entry into a discourse? Is it not rather hearing a word and replying in a word? Now word is not discourse. Both are rooted in language but language is only their common condition of possibility. Word and discourse initiate two heterogeneous and irreducible horizons in language, and, so to speak, lead language in two inevitably divergent directions. Discourse in its proper sense is ordered advance, and thus sequence, and as such binds its listener and its speaker; it acts like a gearing system, in which the mind cannot help but be progressively guided and absorbed. In a sense, discourse is totally given in advance as the immanent logos of the world, present to itself in the form of a self-constituting development. When we become the vehicles of discourse, we do not produce it of ourselves, but re-effect it; we take up in our own intellectual efforts the process of the internal development of discourse. Word introduces discontinuity into experience. Word presents itself as other and remains the other even when heard and recognised. Fixed in its otherness it returns to itself. It does not lead towards other terms, it does not provoke movement. It offers itself in its unity with neither relation nor connexion —a unity which must be taken in its closedness, its irreducibility, its indestructibility, its insularity. Word is linked to event, it itself is event. It is a pure upsurge breaking the continuity of life and of every discourse, surprising all expectation, putting every anticipation in jeopardy. It halts the unfolding of experience and at the same time brings experience back to itself, sets experience over against itself, as a question for itself, as its own burden, as responsibility in regard to itself. As event it is external to our life while at the same time concerning us. It withdraws us from obviousness, challenges us, interrogates us. It is expectation and demand for an answer which can be an answer only when situated in the same dimension—an answer which is itself word. Word brings to be what was not yet. It is newness. It neither repeats, nor re-effects. It creates.

Let us attempt to analyse this first clue. Manifestation and revelation must be distinguished as two fundamental modes of the given. Faith is an attitude towards a revelation. On the other hand, cosmological discourse as the search for correspondence with the cosmos is the interpretation of a reality which is given. But the kind of giving in this case is dissimilar to revelation. The world is given as manifestation and cosmological thought is the explicitation of this manifestation in discourse. What does such a process involve? To become manifest is to become visible, to enter the visible domain, not in the sense of the visual field, but in the sense of an illumined domain within which vision is possible. This entry into visibility is not absolute beginning, it is effected on the basis of a set of conditions which form the horizon of the domain in which the manifestation is produced. It is a complex horizon composed of superimposed interlocking layers in a schema of conditionality. But precisely to the extent that the different layers of the horizon are articulated with respect to each other according to the schema, there will be a unity of conditioning, and a unity in the horizon of conditions. This horizon is also the sphere of the *a priori*. In manifestation the visible thing comes towards us, but its proximity is always conditioned by a distance: it can come close to us only in so far as it is set in the domain of appearance. This domain is an extent, a distancing milieu by virtue of the horizon which surrounds and so posits it. Accordingly the distance in which the manifested thing is held, is its conditioning itself, the givenness of the horizon which allows it appear. Cosmological thought is thought of the manifestation of the cosmos, of the cosmos as manifestation. As thought of origin, of foundation, of that which allows visible things to be as they are, cosmological thought must be linked with manifestation not in its products but in itself. Accordingly, it is thought of manifestation as such, of what constitutes manifestational givenness, of what conditions it, that is of the conditioning horizon which allows the unfolding of the manifestation of space. Manifestation is not passive but active givenness, i.e. operation; the space which it unfolds

is a space of production. This space must be opened for the
visible thing to be produced in its visibility: it is a milieu of
distance but also of illumination. By illuminating what is
produced in it, it reveals the contour of the thing and allows
it to appear according to its form. Within this clarity the
thing stands in its place and its form shines forth in the
context of visibility, emerges in the light of its delimitation
and enters into the glory of its advent. Fixed in its distance
the thing is accessible only through the mediation of separateness. It remains exterior and reaches us only in vision—vision
is the sense of the far away. It gives itself without residue, in
all its faces, all its virtualities, all its profiles, but all the
while it remains in the distance enclosed by the splendour
of its surface; it comes to us, but does not concern us.
Furthermore, if we can meet it, it is because between the
thing and ourselves there is a certain connaturality. For we,
at least in one facet of our being—the facet that brings us
into the visible—are placed in the midst of the world, things
among things.

Revelation is also giving. But the inverse relation between
proximity and distance holds. In manifestation the given
approaches by the intermediary and in virtue of distance. In
revelation the reality which gives itself does so in its distance
by the means of proximity. For what is given in revelation
has common measure neither with us nor with the things
of the world; it is a reality which does not belong to the
cosmos, does not show itself in the cosmos, but holds itself
in impregnable otherness, in a sovereign distance. But this
distance is not the distancing of production, the space opened
by the horizon of conditioning, it is the distance of non-
manifestation, of that from which we are separated by the
opacity of the visible, of the manifestation. What we are
given in revelation is an invisible reality which is given as
invisible. How can such a reality be given effectively? It is
not given as things are given, in person, in the light of
visibility, but in separateness, by the instrument which can
unite absence and presence, which makes absence in its

absence present, namely language. And it is not in its discursive function—that is, inasmuch as it reproduces manifestation—that language is at work here but in the form of an operative word. The word is a term sent forth by the speaker as his delegate, as it were his presence sent outside himself, as making present his distance. As such, the word is operative, since it is mission only to the extent that it makes present, not totally nor exhaustively as the reality that sends it forth is present in itself, but in a way that is perfectible, that initiates a way along which one can endlessly walk. Yet how can speech as word be operative? For it to be active, to accomplish what it contains, it must correspond to a receptivity in us, a place where it can work. In other words it must be able to capitalise on our potentialities and use them to produce itself according to its own nature. It is word only in so far as it seizes us there where we are already given, where it is for us a call which concerns us. In the very movement of concerning itself with us, it commits us. It is call because it is addressed to us as called. It is call because it addresses that demand which comes from the depths of ourselves, because it calls that which in us is vocation or destiny, because it is addressed to that part of ourselves in which we are, continually, a question to ourselves. It is call because it speaks to the domain of our being where this being is decided, where our being appears to itself as possessed of the power and the responsibility to decide about itself. Speech then, meets us not at our periphery but at our centre. For this reason speech is given to be heard and tasted. Hearing and taste are diffuse senses but for this very reason they are the senses of intimacy, interiority, assimilation. If speech can become food, it is because it can be transformed into our substance. Contrariwise, vision is precise; it gives contours which situate and delimit, but for this reason it is a sense of distancing and exteriority. Faith is acceptance of speech, assent to the revealing speech.

The word addressed to that which constitutes us as destiny

is event, disturbance, always new. In this sense it is, truly and absolutely, origin. No doubt discourse, too, refers to an origin, speaks the origin, but in the sense of the originating, i.e. referring to a constituting *a priori*. It may be useful to distinguish originating origin and originated origin. Word is originating origin, pure initiative. Discourse is action of the origin as origin, as already set in motion; it is this setting in motion in its exercise, in its motion, not in what precedes and gives rise to it. Word is older than discourse. Faith introduces the believer into the domain of the word, of the originating origin. It is, thus, beneath (and, by the same token, beyond) discourse in general and cosmological representations in particular. It is inner light, not the light of the external milieu of visibility; illumination of soul not of sight. Faith gets its illuminating power from the word it receives and not at all from the mythic matrix of cosmological discourse. Faith is outside the domain and field of action o myth.

In the words that faith receives, however, there are allusions to cosmological facts through stories of origins and images of the end of time. What, then, is the meaning and intentionality of these images? They are in no sense a presentation of the world, an explanation of its constitution and destiny, they do not compose a cosmological discourse. Quite the contrary, what they envisage is a trans-cosmological meaning in a salvation history. The function of stories of origins is to mark a difference in plane, a rupture between the given world and a domain of reality that is in no sense continuous with the world. These stories tell of a radical otherness; they tell of this world only to go beyond it to a non-world. They are merely instruments of the transition from the given, that is this world, to a trans-cosmological dimension. Their virtue lies in the fact that they relate us to the dimension in which salvation history is constituted and becomes comprehensible, and this dimension is not an element in the system of the cosmos. It neither envelops nor is enveloped by it. The images of the end of time serve to indicate the time of the accomplishment of salvation, of the fullness of revelation. The end will be the moment when at last all the signs through which revelation has been effected will become clear, totally transparent, when what is proclaimed in revelation will be really, immediately and unshakeably present. At this time too, the present figure of the world, already in a certain sense cast aside by the power of the word, will pass away. This is evoked by the images of the final cataclysm and of the sky folded up like a tent. Thus, with respect both to beginning and to end, it is the domain of salvation, the domain in which the word makes itself heard—that is, proclaimed, first in its beginnings and then in its fulfilment. When it speaks of a beginning and of an end of the world, the word speaks of its own beginning and its own consummation. We are faced here with the inverse of a representation of the world. But this implies a duality between what belongs to the cosmos and what is not of the cosmos—that is, between the manifest, the empirical, the visible and that which transcends the visible. With that we return to the foundation and explanation of the duality of discourse and word.

Going beyond world is no longer speculative transcendence. The transcendent reached is not one of constitution, does not go beyond the empirical as its *a priori* condition, is not a transcendental. The *a priori* belongs to the internal structure of reality, it is this world in its texture and in its foundation, it is the cosmos as founded. The other transcendent granted in the word is outside this world. But as this world is our only visible milieu the word comes to us along the way of visibility. It is carried by signs belonging to the visible world. But, unlike discourse, the word includes the possibility of moving beyond the visible. While discourse leads to the foundation of world, the word leads us to that which is, absolutely, origin. While discourse repeats the originated origin, the word reveals the originating origin. All of this is possible only if there is something already in us capable of this true and radical transcendence, capable of grasping the word as word, capable of setting us, as it were, in resonance with originating language. The required dimension must be non-cosmological. We are not open to this dimension as of this world, things among things, but inasmuch as we are open to a constituting call. The receptive dimension in which the word's way begins in us is an ethical dimension.

What then, is to be said of the relation between word and cosmos, or—and this comes to the same thing inasmuch as the operation constitutive of the cosmos is itself discourse—between word and discourse? Basically the relation is of the originating origin to the originated origin. Revelation, in the word it speaks to us, presents this relation by its use of the symbolism of the word; so the originating word symbolises itself by itself, by the revealing word. The originating origin is spoken of as word, and the end is spoken of as advent, as the total revelation of the Word. Thus word is originating with respect to cosmos and so to discourse. None the less, the word, in that it addresses us and that in it we are enabled to answer its call, relies on language and must borrow from language part of its meaning, even if it does so in order to evoke a new meaning. To the extent that it employs cosmological representations, e.g. terms like 'life', 'space', 'origin', 'antecedence', it introduces meanings previously established in discourse. But if word speaks otherwise than discourse, and says something other than discourse, these meanings must be transformed utterly. At the conclusion of the transformation, word may bear these meanings in itself but as transcended, as the context on which it had, partially and in passing, to rely in order to gain that domain which is radically beyond that context.

How is such transformation possible? Will it not be by borrowing from another source of meaning, which is also bound to an effectuation although not that of the cosmos, namely life understood as destiny and meeting? When one life is face to face with another life, when the two cross each other's path as destinies, they make of each other a twofold challenge, the challenge of self by self and the challenge of self by the other. Each one challenging the other is, at the same time, challenged by the other. This dimension of destiny refers back to an initiating source in which existence is put in question and puts itself in question. Within this dimension meeting takes place. Meeting is emergence, newness; it constitutes itself as expectation of aid and as call. The other, given in meeting, appears as the custodian of the key to the place where a life can take off. The other is likewise demand to the extent that he lets it be understood, in his giving of himself, that the person who receives the gift, in his turn, holds the key to the existence of the giver. The first experience which nourishes the significative power of the word is in this confrontation that is meeting, in the challenge which both constitutes us and put us into question.

(*b*) *From discourse to faith*: We may conclude with a consideration of the second question. If between discourse and word the relation just discussed obtains, is there within discourse itself an indication of a possible way to faith, an orientation towards faith? If word is rooted in the ethical dimension and can in virtue of this raise the cosmological representations through a metamorphosis of meaning beyond the cosmic milieu, may it not be possible to give an ethical reinterpretation of the cosmological?

A more profound analysis than is possible at this point is required to answer these questions adequately. However, some brief notes are in order. To deal properly with the question one would have to consider certain problems raised, or as least suggested, by science, especially by the most recent advances of science. One thinks at once of such problems as those of origin, indeterminism, irreversibility. Cosmological physics endeavours to provide some representation of the origin whether in the form of a primitive atom, an undifferentiated state preceding the differentiating process which results in the present world, or in the form of a continuous creation whose function is to maintain the density of matter in the universe constant by affording the required compensation to the recession of nebulae. Quantum physics, on the level of microphysical phenomena, has revealed an indeterminism whose role seems essential. (No doubt it seems possible to reinterpret quantum physics within the framework of a deterministic theory but a theory of this kind would inevitably require chance processes at a sub-quantum level.) It may be asked if the indetermination in question is subjective or objective, i.e. if it is merely a consequence of our ignorance of the parameters which determine the phenomena which to us seem aleatory, or if in fact it is an intrinsic characteristic of physical reality. If one attributes an entirely objective character to the indetermination one is led to the conclusion that there is in nature something not-caused. How is this to be accounted for? It is not enough to invoke an initial chance distribution which has evolved in a determined manner through time, for there are continually new chance distributions. In other words, even if one begins with an initial distribution one has to introduce chance modifications of the resulting configurations. This seems to suggest that there is at work in nature a spontaneity which is beyond physical thought. Finally, nature as a whole seems to present an irreversibility due to the incessant interactions of the parts of the universe, which manifests itself as a progressive dissipation of order. M. O. Costa de Beauregard has put forward an interpretation of this fact based on the equivalence between neg-entropy (entropy with the sign reversed) and information suggested by Léon Brillouin. As an increase of entropy corresponds to an increase of disorder, so a diminution of entropy, i.e. an increase in negentropy, corresponds to an increase of order and a given amount of order may be thought of as a given amount of information. Thus one arrives at a general principle of conservation in the form of the conservation of the sum, negentropy plus information. If there is progressive loss of negentropy it must be compensated for by an accumulation of information in a region inaccessible to experimental physics. The end may be represented in M. Costa de

Beauregard's bold image as a reinfusion into the universe of all this accumulated information, like a vast 'implosion of finality' (contrasting with the dissipation of negentropy which is an explosion).

Of what significance are these questions suggested by contemporary science? From the scientific viewpoint it is difficult to go beyond whatever is contained in their exact formulation or the formulation of associated hypotheses. But from the philosophic viewpoint it might be legitimate to interpret them as signs of lacunae in the fabric of manifestation, and of the presence in manifestation of a reasonableness that cannot be eliminated. Assuming that an interpretation could be developed along these lines, can one see in it a real transcendence of discourse and manifestation? All desire of transcendence would still be rooted in the project of 'accounting for' according to the logic of discourse, according to the demands of manifestation. By recognising in the light of this desire the fact that the lacunae are not to be eliminated, one is in effect calling a halt, marking a limit whose meaning would be: if there is a reason, it is not a reason that speculative intelligence could recognise; if there is some way of assigning a reason, it is no longer in the form of a reason.

Perhaps there are ways of bypassing this desire, this project of 'accounting for', of trying not to 'go beyond' the lacunae but to move from their disclosure to a dimension which would be no longer explanation but reception, a dimension of acceptance, revelation, faith. The displacement is possible, if at all, only by relying, in advance, on this new dimension. And if it is founded on the ethical dimension of our existence, it will consist in a reinterpretation of the lacunae in the light of ethics—that is, in understanding them as bearers of indications pointing towards ethics. But how can a lacuna in manifestation indicate the direction of ethical intention?

The mere acknowledgement of lacunae can lead only to a philosophy of spontaneity. Science allows us to understand only the general regularities of the universe—that is, whatever can be expressed in the form of systems of relations endowed with sufficient stability. Science rests on a general principle of causality which is, in the last analysis, a principle of stability. The equations describing the behaviour of the universe must not contain functions that change their form in the course of time. Along the lines suggested by this principle, representations are constructed and laws formulated, whether determinist or statistical. (Statistical laws do not govern the behaviour of isolated systems but the behaviour of statistical aggregates formed from isolated systems.) However, this representation is an abstraction and cannot return to the concrete—that is, to actual manifestation. There are in nature hierarchical levels of organisation and each one represents with respect to its predecessor a highly improbable state. And internal to each level there are local and individual determinations which seem to be a-causal. Accordingly, a principle of operation is required which is not to be grasped on the level of phenomena and which can be represented by a model of liberty. What is required is a spontaneity, an inventive activity, which truly introduces novelty, and within the chains of law heralds the advent of the improbable. A spontaneity of this kind is finalisation and also creation of forms according to a principle of the better analogous to the principle of the platonic demiurge. It is the emergence of harmony, of ever more perfect forms of unification.

What is the value of a representation such as this? In the first place, by disclosing the lacunae in manifestation and the irreducible inadequacy of a complete representation of the world in the mode of constitution, it frees us from the fascination which is inevitably exercised by the vision of the manifest in so far as it appears to us in its perfection, its achievement and its clarity. In the second place, it associates the internal movement of nature with the internal movement of human existence inasmuch as it elicits the discovery in both of a real inventiveness. Of course, the spontaneity of

13

the life of forms is not yet liberty but it is at least an *analogon* of liberty and offers an understanding of liberty, of the experiences made possible by its emergence.

Is there not, when we read it sufficiently profoundly, an analogy between the deep structure of nature and the structure of human existence as openness, creativity, possibility of accord with the event? The problematic of nature can thus be linked with the problematic of human existence. Still there is not a continuity between the two domains. There are perhaps indications pointing in a certain direction but it is not within the power of cosmological thought, even when developed to become a consideration of finality, to enter the domain of the word. Only by meditating on what properly belongs to word can one open another way of understanding (if one exists), leading towards, but never actually reaching, faith.

Conclusion

The Problematic of the Language of Faith

THE location of the language of faith within the order of the spoken word indicates three characteristics (at least) which contribute to determining its structure: it relates to events, it implies a commitment, it includes an eschatological reference. The words of faith evoke a reality which is in process, namely salvation as presented in the teachings of Christ and the Apostles. Inasmuch as it is a work, an action which unfolds in history, salvation is in itself an event, not in the sense of a sudden shift discernible in a temporal flux but in the sense of an enduring constitutive process coextensive with history. This persistently unfolding event is composed of a complex chain of actions in which arise individual, historically situated events marking the several moments of divine intervention in human living. These events are organised with respect to a central set of events which is the life, death and resurrection of Christ. The events of the Old Testament prepare and prefigure Christ's accomplishment. And in the passage of time the life of the Church unfolds what Christ proclaims and has already realised. But this life too is a figure of what is to come. For the Christian, life is understood as hope.

Faith is the acceptance and the ratification of what revelation proposes. In this respect it would seem that the language of faith could be assimilated into a theoretic language: it appears to be made up of propositions of the constative type which affirm, from the outside so to speak, certain 'truths' about the inward nature of God and about the relations between God and man. But on closer inspection it appears that the content of the affirmations of faith relates neither to the properties of God considered as a sort of strange object, nor to the God–man relation, considered as objective, but relates rather to that which, on God's part and on man's, concerns the realisation of the divine plan in man, the alliance foretold to the patriarchs and sealed in the mystery of Christ, the assumption of humanity into the life of God. Put another way, the affirmations of faith bear on what is in process of realisation in the being of the believer. For all that, they are not simply descriptive propositions: they are neither a 'theory' of salvation, nor a 'theory of the nature of God'. The affirmations of faith are not foreign to the achievement they express. On the contrary, they are part of that achievement. By making these affirmations the believer is making his answer to the proposition told him in preaching; thus he takes up in himself and for himself the movement of salvation. What is said in the affirmations of faith is, then, precisely that which is accomplished by means of the affirmations. The language of faith is self-involving from two viewpoints: from the viewpoint of acts and from the viewpoint of contents. By taking up in himself the affirmations of faith the believer achieves an act which concerns himself and modifies his being. Further, these affirmations, by becoming operative in virtue of this existential involvement of the believer, bring about what they say. In their content they concern the operations whose instruments they are.

Now the language of faith can have these characteristics to the extent that it bears on events. An event brings about a new state of affairs; it brings an operative power into play. The events referred to in faith are not simply historical incidents. They are always in act because they fit in to one great event that is in process of realisation. This event animates the word of faith and makes of this word an event, makes it operative. Its efficacy is in virtue of the event of which it speaks. So we can understand how in this word the

content of what is said and the underlying operation can
coincide.

As the language of faith does nor properly become what
it is, namely a language of accomplishment or realisation,
except to the extent that it is taken up into an act of
ratification (signified by the 'I believe'), it is bound up with
commitment. It is the involvement of the believer in the
words he speaks which gives these words their efficacy,
their power to realise what they signify. Because in his word
the believer brings his consent to the work of salvation that
the word of faith proclaims, this work is effectively present
in his word and active in him. The event constituting the
affirmation of faith and in which the believer's commitment
is enacted is, then, a coincidence of two operations: first, an
act of willing which recognises in the signs (preaching, the
Christian life, the Church, and through these, the life of
Christ) the invitation addressed to him and accepts the
gift of God; secondly, this gift itself represented in the word
but at the same time acting within it and sustaining through
it the receptive will.

Nevertheless, faith speaks of an event yet to come. What
is proclaimed in the life and preaching of Christ, what is
signified in his death, and attested in his resurrection is a
mystery, that is a hidden reality, which is yet visible enough
for hearts unbiased by the prestige of wisdom and power to
recognise, but still present only enigmatically. In attesting
this reality, faith discloses at once the clarity and the mystery.
The language of faith, then, harbours an inner tension. It
points to a reality, recognised through signs, whose active
presence it affirms. Yet it represents this reality as yet to
come, as the unbounded term of a journey whose length is
not yet fixed. It is in so far as he relies on what the available
signs give him in the present that the believer can assume,
as it were in advance, the reality that is to come. And it is
in so far as he refers himself to this reality that he becomes
capable of understanding in the given signs what he recognises there. He therefore doubly refers himself to salvation;

on the one hand as actively present in human life, on the other hand as final event, held in suspense in the future. This final term is not an object of representation, it is rather the substance of what is now lived; the present is the earnest of the future. It is in the word's actuality that the message it carries within it is disclosed. In its actuality, the coming for which it hopes is prepared. Once again it is because the language of faith has to do with events that it is related in its actuation to an 'eschaton'. The structure of this reference is that of the event itself; inasmuch as it is in preparation, through signs and figures, salvation is at once the unceasing achievement of and the unceasing wait for itself. In the 'eschaton' it becomes total but this becoming total is operative in the here and now. Because it is revelation—that is, the advent of the presence of God—it is both visible and hidden, fully attested and at the same time object of hope. The language of faith is a language of hope. As such it is doubly commitment: not only does it recognise the saving word in what is proclaimed, but it also affirms itself as already bound by the promise brought by that word.

We may fairly claim, then, that the language of faith is, in all its aspects, performative. Still this is only one of its dimensions of meaning. It includes a 'constative' aspect; it affirms certain propositions as true (e.g. God's existence, the Trinity, the divinity of Christ, the mission of the Church). Of course these propositions could be interpreted as performatives. So for instance one could take the proposition 'I believe in God' as no more than an expression of an *attitude* of submission and confidence. But a proposition of this kind is nonsensical if the person affirming it does not in fact believe that there is a God in whom he can have confidence and to whose will he must submit. Accordingly, even if one interpreted the propositions of the language of faith entirely in terms of attitudes, one would still have to recognise that they implied existential constative propositions. Now it seems to be more in conformity with the nature of faith to attribute a constative dimension to these propositions directly.

This means that these propositions rely—at least for part of their meaning—on a criterion of truth. Can this criterion be precisely formulated? As faith speaks of an invisible reality there can be no question of an empiricist criterion. One might, of course, claim that this reality was referred to only through the intermediary of certain signs (the historical Christ, the Church as a visible community, for example) which have the status of historical objects accessible through documents and testaments and that, accordingly, the proper criterion was of the kind adequate to historical objects. However, what is clearly essential is the relation which links these objects to the realities of which they are the signs, and here the criteria of historical language are obviously inadequate. Perhaps one might call on metaphysical language. But even if this language did not bristle with all too well known difficulties, it is hard to admit that the language of faith should be judged by criteria borrowed from metaphysics. Furthermore, allowing that metaphysics was successful in demonstrating God's existence, how could it be of any help with the Trinity or Christ's divinity? Perhaps we should look for criteria based on attitudes, e.g. that the truth of affirmations of faith is guaranteed by the dispositions and behaviour inspired by faith. But this would be to return by another route to an exclusively performative interpretation.

It does not seem that the available criteria provide an adequate solution to our problem. The language of faith has its own criteria and a correct analysis of this language should be able to reveal them. Now the only way of tackling this problem that remains to us is to attempt first to resolve the question of the mode of meaning of the language of faith. Now if it is not possible to reduce the semantic of this language entirely to a theory of performatives, then it becomes imperative to study the language from the viewpoint of the relation of signification, that is according to the semantic categories of reference, denotation, connotation and use. Here the self-involving character of the language of faith raises special problems. There are many language forms that speak of realities inaccessible in practice, and even in principle, to perception. In the matter of a theoretic language the very function of the language indicates how its terms behave semantically; in other words it is possible to discover the meaning of these terms by an examination of the links which the theory itself establishes between them and certain other terms relative to realities that can be empirically grasped. But the language of faith cannot be compared to a theoretic language; not only does it not have an explanatory function with regard to sense experience, but it is the language itself and only the language which presents the realities of which it speaks. It speaks of that which operates in it. Are we not here confined in a circle from which there is no issue? Is it not the case that the language of faith is purely and simply self-referential? Is it not the case that its referential force is simply confounded with its performativity?

The answer to this question presupposes further precision of the notion of performativity. In the affirmation of faith there is certainly an active commitment on the speaker's part. It is also true that this commitment is the correlative of the work of salvation referred to in the language of faith and taken up by the believer in his commitment. But if it is true that it is in virtue of the work of salvation that the believer accepts faith, it does not follow that what is said in the language of faith is identical with the commitment by which it becomes operative. In other words, we must distinguish the operation spoken of in the language of faith from the operation in virtue of which that language is produced. Naturally, the two operations are related—as faith affirms—but they are none the less distinct. Further, the question in hand has to do with the language of faith as language and not with the movement of salvation. The language which speaks of salvation is not itself salvation. Its performativity is a linguistic property and not the saving action that it signifies and that transforms the believer into

someone capable of accepting that salvation. The performativity of the language of faith is the property it possesses as
language of giving effect to certain attitudes proper to the
believer (e.g. acceptance, ratification, confidence). This
property should not be confused with the salvific efficacy of
which the language can be an instrument, when, for example
it becomes the sign of the birth, in the soul of the believer,
of what it proclaims. Accordingly, strictly from the viewpoint of an analysis of language, one is led to discover that
the performativity of the language of faith does not exhaust
its meaning, that its content is not coincident with its
effectuation, that it includes a referential relation that bears
analysis.

At this point the relevance of hermeneutics becomes
apparent. For the language of faith speaks of realities which
are not, as such, perceptible. Doubtless it appeals to 'signs'—
events through which the divine plan, to which it finally
refers, is disclosed. These signs, in so far as they are situations, events, persons, words, can be related to perceptions
either directly or indirectly through testimony and historical
tradition. For instance, the tradition transmitted in the
community of the Church points to the experience of the
first Christian community. But in the language of faith
there is something quite beyond this evocation of a form of
life realised at a given time by a determinate group of
people. This form of life itself is understood as attesting to
a non-visible event, namely the revelation of God in Jesus
Christ. What is peculiar to the language of faith is the grasp
of the sign as sign—that is, the discovery in the sign of the
invisible reality which it proclaims or presents. In this sense
it is already a hermeneutic: it comprises an interpretation of
the signs of salvation. This will be the case to the extent that
it presents in its expressions the reality to which the signs
point. As this reality is not visible it will be impossible to
explain the meaning of the terms denoting or determining
it by recourse to ostension (which would consist in *showing*
the referent of the terms or in presenting objects in which

14

the properties which the terms denote would be verified). The envisaged meaning has to be suggested by using terms whose meaning can be determined either directly or indirectly by means of such procedures. (Direct determination occurs when the term itself can be explained by indicating an appropriate object. There will be indirect determination when the term in question can be related, through a series of meaningful propositions, to directly determinable terms, in other words, when the term can be defined, explicitly or contextually, by means of terms of the first type.)

The semantic functioning of language provides the necessary resources. On the level of ordinary language we discover *figuration* procedures. These consist in using a term in an unusual sense but in such a way that this sense can be understood on the basis of already established senses. An easily analysed figurative usage of language is metaphor where the second (non-usual) sense is linked to the first (already established) sense by similarity. Of course, in general it is impossible to give exact and totally unambiguous specifications of the invoked resemblance. Still, it is always possible to *explicate* a metaphor, that is to make explicit the relation between the first and second sense. This operation implies the possibility of an independent characterisation of the second sense, the possibility of separating the two senses.

The language of faith makes use of certain terms (e.g. 'father', 'son', 'life', 'kingdom', 'heaven', etc) in a figurative sense. The envisaged meaning, which is a derivative sense of the term, cannot be adequately elucidated except by relying on a sense already constituted on a level of a language other than that of faith. So it is not merely a question of a metaphor. May we talk of symbols? It depends on how the term is understood. A symbol may be characterised as follows: it is a term with a twofold reference such that the derived referential relation, which envisages the reality denoted, is not separable from the first referential relation given in the non-symbolic usage of the term. Still the language of faith is not adequately described by saying that it has recourse to a symbolic usage of its expressions. We have to discover precisely how the second sense is linked to the first, and the import and justification of this link, its specificity and to what extent the envisaged meaning remains closed to an autonomous elucidation which would make the link redundant.

These questions may be approached from two different perspectives. One way would be to ask how this transcending of meaning, which, following the direction indicated by the semantic structure of the expressions used in the language of faith, leads towards the reality they intend, takes place. A second way would be to propose an elucidation of the second sense in terms of a different yet appropriate language, for example scientific or speculative language. In the first instance the elucidation would consist in a description of the intended reality in terms of an accepted theory, say, of affectivity or a sociological theory. In the second instance, it would consist in a description of this reality in terms of an anthropological or ontological interpretation, say, within the framework of a philosophy of existence, or of a philosophy of history, or of a metaphysical theory of the absolute, or of a discourse on being. An elucidation of this kind could respect the symbolic character of the language of faith. There would be no question of reducing its terms to mere metaphors by showing that the two meanings could be separated from each other; the crucial thing would be to show how and why the language of faith had necessarily to take the form of a symbolic language in the strict sense. And it would be quite possible to do this while still putting forward a 'reductionist' interpretation whether scientific, existential or ontological. It would be enough to introduce a distinction between naïve and critical consciousness and to show that it belonged to the nature of the reality explained on the level of critical consciousness to appear to naïve consciousness only in the mode of symbolic representation. The language of faith would thus be interpreted as an expression of naïve consciousness. And its role in history could be elucidated by showing that in certain conditions consciousness was necessarily naïve.

However, one may wonder if an interpretation of this kind is not too easy in its willingness to accept wholeheartedly the framework of some privileged language and to reduce the language of faith to a mechanism which can be wholly explained within the terms of the selected language. One may, of course, note that the language of faith is not critical, at least not as scientific and philosophic discourse are critical, but this does not suffice to justify the reductive approach. The fact that a language has a critical form is not sufficient to give it the status of a fundamental language with authority over all others. But in every reductionist attempt it is presupposed, either explicitly or implicitly, that the complete system of all possible meanings is necessarily coterminous with the system of meanings that can be made explicit in a given language which is considered as regulative. It seems hard to discover an argument to justify this presupposition.

Should we not rather admit that there is in the language of faith a specific modality of meaning and that this specificity needs to be articulated? For it is only after we have analysed it in its own intentionality that we could show that it depends in the end on an 'elucidation' in another language. But if we posit in advance that it *must* be elucidated in a privileged language, then we preclude even the possibility of its revealing what is proper to it. Faith must be allowed speak in its own language if we are to understand how it speaks. We are thus led to retain only a hermeneutic in the first sense, namely an analysis of the mode of semantic breakthrough proper to the language of faith (rather than a transcription of this language into another).

What, then, is the precise task of a hermeneutic understood in this way? What is the orientation suitable to an analysis of the language of faith? One must begin by showing the possibility of the semantic going-beyond that it effects. Then we must show how it makes a sign towards that about which it speaks, how it enlightens and, finally, how it includes an orientation towards truth. To show how the language of faith is possible we must indicate the dimension within which the reality is situated—that is, the reality which its proper sense intends and which appears as derived as long as the language is regarded as symbolic. Now this dimension must, inasmuch as it is a condition of possibility, precede the event expressed in the language of faith and so it may be expressed in a different language, for instance, a speculative one. Perhaps ethical language is more suited to the task, for its function is to describe human existence as destiny—that is, as not yet accomplished but as able to accomplish itself and as capable of concerning itself with what it is called to be. In his ethical dimension man appears as a demand which is nothing else than the modality according to which his own being discloses itself as not equal to himself and as calling forth a development in which he will be given to himself in truth, in the taking up and the breaking down of the distance separating him from himself. He appears in relation to this exigence as depending on his own initiative. He is not an objective process, he is his own becoming, that is a staking of himself on his own action. He must himself posit the content that will replace the void of the demand by the effectiveness of what is accomplished. There is a task which defines him as an ethical being: to achieve coincidence between the deep movement of his being—the willing which constitutes him—and the effective reality which he gives himself in his acting. But the exact nature of the demand that he is remains an enigma: it can be disclosed only piecemeal in his effort to make his life correspond with it. His content is not given in advance but posits itself in the achievement called forth in the demand. The demand, then, is a horizon, a field of possibility, constitutive but not determined. As such he can be the locus of revelation—that is, the locus for revelation to establish a space for its unfolding. In terms of language this means that ethical language can describe the region from which there is access to the reality spoken of in the language of faith. Inasmuch as ethical language speaks of destiny it points, as it were, to an anticipatory form to which salvation will bring a determinate content. As the dimension of the destiny is already non-perceivable and so requires a speculative language, it provides the ground of the possibility of a language which speaks of the non-visible.

Yet this is but a preliminary step in the analysis. The real work is the attempt to characterise the semantic articulation proper to the language of faith. Now this is something quite distinct from a speculative language for it is at the same time a language of truth and commitment. The introduction of the 'I believe' is indicative of a step which is both acknowledgement and position, which enlightens only to the extent that it ratifies and in which, accordingly, will and perception are conjoint. Only mediated by the commitment that it expresses does the language of faith reveal the reality that it invokes, because the reality is presented only for this commitment which concerns precisely what is affirmed in faith. The word of faith does not consist in expressing a subjective adherence to a certain number of propositions but in binding the speaker, in an act of radical confidence, to the self-revealing word, and in making him receptive of what is revealed. The self-revealing word is God himself inasmuch as he calls man to share his life and what is revealed is the the mystery of this adoption— that is, God in his plan in man's regard and in his saving act. So it is truly itself that the revealing word reveals. The act of confidence bears on the same reality that faith recognises. The 'I believe' is both adherence to the word of God inasmuch as man is addressed, and recognition of what this word discloses of itself in that invitation.

The expression of faith properly refers to the content of the revealing word (God as Father, Son and Spirit. As Father, by the mediation of the Spirit, calling men to accept the condition of sons by incorporating themselves in the Son, made man, and come to dwell among us). The expressions of faith have this power of reference from the commitment which underlies them. It is not, therefore, simply a question of calling forth in a symbolic language a reality that could be grasped in some other way independently of the language in intuition and sentiment. Nor is it a matter of describing a problematic reality in the symbolic mode. Here language plays an irreplaceable mediating role which presents what it speaks of. It is in the words it speaks that the concrete form proposed to human destiny in the revelation of salvation receives a structure and so can be grasped and understood. It is in these words that it takes on a particular aspect and so becomes effectively inspiring. The words use terms that have an already established sense on the level of ordinary language. But the illocutionary force of the words of faith, the commitment that holds them and to which they give form, gives another meaning to the ordinary terms. In the symbolism of faith the intended meaning is not really a derived meaning; it is rather constitutive. It is not the first sense that allows the second sense to be understood. It is rather that the second sense transvalues the first by giving the terms an entirely new meaning. Yet we cannot say, for all that, that any term whatsoever will serve as a support for this transvaluation. For there is in the first sense of the terms used a receptivity and an openness which make them apt foundations for the structuring of meaning instituted by the word of faith. And in this sense we may say that it is in the direction in which the first sense points that the second sense can emerge. The act of faith is the condition of its emergence. Yet the first sense calls it forth.

The language of faith refers to a reality which is not given except in the language itself, and which appears only in it. And this reality is disclosed in the language only inasmuch as the language is itself an act in which the believer welcomes that which his word speaks. The language does not restrict itself to a (symbolic) description of the properties of its referents, to a discussion about them, rather it discloses these referents themselves in what it says of them. Still this does not imply that its meaning is fixed once and for all. It should not be forgotten that it is the correlative of an experience: bound itself to attitudes, it is called forth by certain movements and it in turn calls forth certain initiatives. Faith always presupposes a quest; the faithful word is preceded by interrogation, expectation, presentiment; it demands a change of heart. There is always a prelude to the word. And on the other hand, faith demands works and holiness. The experience that goes along with faith is that of journeying; the action by which the believer accepts salvation is also a waiting for salvation—the sketch only of its fulfilment. Faith is not a saturated vision, it is open to an eschatological horizon, it is bound up with hope.

The language of faith is revealing only in a mode of ceaseless deepening. From the time the believing word is truly spoken it brings into presence and act what it speaks of, it brings into the space it constitutes the mystery that it evokes and so discloses it. It says what it discloses: to this extent it depends on 'constative' language. But what is shown is always at the same time concealed; what is disclosed remains hidden. Faith illuminates not by showing in the clarity of an image, but by making understood in openness of heart—that is, in the attitude of acceptance and ratification that its word implies. There is, then, inseparable solidarity between vision and attitude: the believer sees what his word proclaims in so far as he is open to the power of the revealing word, and, reciprocally, what he sees gives him the power to open himself to what is proposed. This is no mere correlation of two aspects. The language of faith is the place of a ceaseless going beyond: the more complete the commitment becomes, the clearer the vision becomes and if the mystery never ceases to be mystery it yet continues to reveal undreamt-of depths. There is an infinity in the language of faith; it reveals while remaining open to a more illuminating revelation. It does not, however, abandon its reliance on the same expressions; but what it means it can always more adequately mean. In other words, the movement of going beyond, that brings the object of faith within the scope of its language, gives to the language its symbolising force and articulates meaning in it as eductive, is an unceasing movement, an illumination which does not stop at a meaning once given but always brings a new and a true way of seeing.

It is perhaps by exploring more closely and deeply the connexion between the performative and the demonstrative aspects of the language of faith that we can understand, at least to a certain extent, how that language signifies and, underlying this as a foundation, in what sense it depends on a criterion of truth. If the language of faith is linked to a progression both in its internal structure and in the works which prolong it, it must be able to include in its movement the guarantees of its truth. These guarantees cannot consist in a confrontation between propositions and constatations, but in the mode according to which the object of the propositions of faith discloses itself. If this object is not given save by the mediation of the word of faith, then this word must contain internally the criteria of its truth, which does not imply that it must indicate a process of verification which can be undertaken at will. What is implied is that it is in itself the process of its own unceasing verification. The word of faith verifies itself in its realisation and it appears to itself as perpetually more true the deeper it becomes. By steeping himself in faith the believer sees with continual adequacy what is revealed. Again this does not imply that in the experience of faith there is not a core of darkness. Nor does it imply that what is disclosed can be expressed in terms other than the simple words of a confession of faith. For it is the characteristic of mystery to be unfathomable in its revelation.

We must not forget that the progression of faith joins action to the word, that it is impossible to separate works from what language proclaims, and that the latter is verified as much in the acts it inspires as in its own realisation. The word of faith constitutes itself as true by becoming increasingly effective. The true criterion is the coherence of a life, its content, its realisation, the extent to which it makes visible the work of salvation—that is, the extent to which holiness is manifest in it. Such a criterion, indeed, is neither definable in canonical terms, nor ever compelling. It is decisive for anyone who carries out the test, however implicitly, in himself. But considered from the outside, it remains ineluctably problematic. Holiness is of the order of witness not demonstration: a sign, not a proof. It raises a question; it does not necessarily give an answer.

So the language of faith is such that it is impossible, without betraying it, either to define absolutely clearly and unequivocally its mode of meaning, or to provide its claims to truth in such a way as to be beyond dispute. Its status is problematic, not in the sense that it escapes analysis, but in the sense that it imposes on analysis a seemingly unending task. Dedication to clarity must not run counter to fidelity to the object. And the clarity of the word is not the clarity of discourse. The language of analysis is the language of discursivity. The language of faith is that of presence. It is language because it articulates its semantic field by using the resources of natural language but it gets its specific signifying power from the act of acknowledgement which constitutes it and which is itself acceptance of a self-giving word. This is why, if it illuminates it does so enigmatically but also in the mode of promise. What it proclaims it proclaims as to be hoped for. 'Faith is the pledge of the good we hope for, the proof of realities which we do not see.'

Acknowledgements

I. Signs and Concepts in Science. Presented at a conference organised by the Secretariat International des Questions Scientifiques du Mouvement International des Intellectuels Catholiques on the topic 'Methodology of research in science and theology', Rome 1968. Published in the proceedings of the conference in the collection *Recherches et Débats* of the Centre Catholique des Intellectuels Français, *Science et théologie, Méthode et langage*, Paris: Desclée De Brouwer, 1970, pp. 107–29.

II. Symbolism as Domain of Operations. Presented at a conference organised by the Société de Symbolisme at Brussels, November 1962 and published in the *Cahiers Internationaux de Symbolisme* (Havré-lez-Mons, Belgique), no 3, 1963.

III. The Neo-Positivist Approach. The present text is practically the whole of an article published in the *Revue des Questions Scientifiques* (Louvain), XXV, 1964 under the title 'Athéisme et neo-positivisme'. That article in its turn is an abridged version of a study entitled 'Ateismo e neo-positivismo' published in *L'ateismo contemporaneo*, II, Turin: Società Editrice Internazionale, 1968, pp. 399–450.

IV. Self-involving Language, Theology and Philosophy. The text in this translation is different from that in the original. The first part is translated from an article published in the *Revue Philosophique de Louvain*, vol. 65, 1967, pp. 115–21. The second part (Questions arising out of Evans' theory) is translated from the main work and forms part of an article

204   *Language and Belief*

which appeared in the *Tijdschrift voor Filosofie* (Louvain), vol. 28, 1966. This article is a fuller version of a talk given in Dutch during a work-shop organised at Louvain, 6 and 7 May 1966, by the 'Wijsgerig Gezelschap te Leuven' on analytical philosophy.

V. Determinism and Responsibility: The Language of Action. Originally published in the *Revue des Questions Scientifiques* (Louvain), vol. 140, January 1969. This was a revised version of a talk given in Paris in March 1968 during a conference organised by the *Union Catholiques des Scientifiques Français*, on the subject 'Determinism and Responsibility'.

VI. Science, Philosophy and Faith. Published in *Le doute et la foi*, no. 61 in the collection *Recherches et Débats* of the Centre Catholique des Intellectuels Français, Paris: Desclée De Brouwer, 1967.

VII. Faith and Cosmology. Presented at a Conference organised in January 1966 at Rome by the Centro Internazionale di studi Umanistici and by the Instituto di studi Filosofici di Roma. Published in the Proceedings: *Mythe et Foi*, ed. Enrico Castelli, Paris: Editions Aubier-Montaigne, 1966.